# Picture Perfect Business Success

*How to Go from Confusion*

*To Clarity in Your Business*

*By*

*Paul Hatrak, CPA,CGMA*

Copyright© 2018 Paul Hatrak

Published and distributed by 30 Day Bestseller, LLC

All rights reserved. No part of this book may be reproduced by any mechanical, photographic, or electronic process, or in the form of a phonographic recording; nor may it be stored in a retrieval system, transmitted, or otherwise be copied for public or private use – other than for 'fair use' as brief quotations embodied in articles and reviews – without prior written permission of the author.

Jimmy,

Wishing You

Picture Perfect

Success!

Paul

# Picture Perfect Business Success

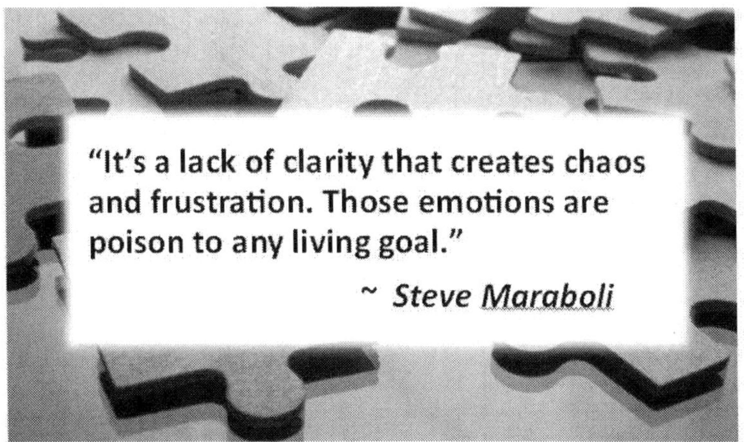
"It's a lack of clarity that creates chaos
and frustration. Those emotions are
poison to any living goal."
~ Steve Maraboli

**Picture Perfect Business Success**

Picture Perfect Business Success

**Special thanks to**

Wife, Sandy

Parents, Paul and Josephine

In-laws, John and Lorraine

Brother, Michael

Sister, Josephine (Jay) and her husband Rob and children Mario and Nina

Brother-in-law, Allan and his wife Denise and daughter Ariella

College CPA friends King's Boys '85: Scott Jenkins, Joseph Killian, John Loyack, Robert Thomas

Mentors: Networking Expert Martin Latman, CPA, The Landing Expert Alex Freund, Branding Expert Pegine Echevarria, Certified Business Coach Margaret Maclay, Construction CPA Jerome Killian, CPA

Editor Extraordinaire, Lawrence Coven

Experts in their respective fields:

LinkedIn: Julbert Abraham and Kim Pearlstein

Marketing: Mindy Scarlett

Publisher: Chris Kelly

National Speakers Association (NSA): Tommy "Toolbox" Hilcken and Sheryl Bindelglass

Commercial Insurance, Alfred Marquis and Leslie Nylund

Title Insurance, Bernie Pane

Certified Wealth Strategist, Walter Pardo

Financial Advisor, Samuel Soprano

Others too numerous to mention...

# Table of Contents

# Forward

I come from a long line of family members who are self-employed, so it was a natural progression for me to step out of the corporate culture and into my own business. However, looking at a business from the outside is a far cry from experiencing it from within!

As I began to navigate through the maze of establishing a business I began to realize that the model of my family was actually one of self-employment, not one of creating and growing a business.

I had to learn the hard way that wearing all the hats was the recipe for monumental stress and potential financial disaster. I had to learn the hard way that a true business is about leverage, about systems and creating teams that work synergistically together. (I am still trying to learn the art of delegating . . .)

What I had to learn the hard way, you now have the chance to learn from Picture Perfect Business Success. This book is full of practical, real world advice that will give you a 'leg up' on how to create the clarity that you need to make your business successful.

Paul Hatrak has provided a basic, easy to read guidebook on how to create your 'picture on the box' so that putting together your business puzzle becomes as easy as 1-2-3. Take advantage of all the great advice and have fun on your journey to clarity!

Mindy Scarlett

*Mindy Scarlett is the Managing Director of The Scarlett Consulting Group, a boutique marketing agency in central New Jersey. Her area of expertise is helping newly minted entrepreneurs get started the right way.*

# Section One

## Purpose – Determining Your Why

# Chapter One

## The Need for Clarity

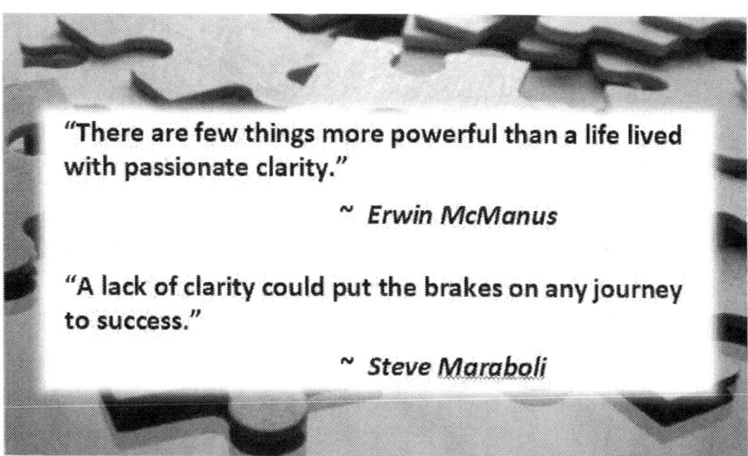

"There are few things more powerful than a life lived with passionate clarity."
~ Erwin McManus
"A lack of clarity could put the brakes on any journey to success."
~ Steve Maraboli

The concept of owning a business is as American as baseball and apple pie. The American Dream was established by our Founding Fathers when they launched the revolutionary idea that a person's pursuit of their own happiness was not self-indulgent, but a necessary force to create the entrepreneurial spirit that defines our free-market economy.

Since that time, millions of Americans have lived their dream of starting their own business. They have taken a passion and turned it into a way to make a living. Almost 90% of Americans work for small businesses (20 employees or less) making small business essential to the workforce and the overall economy.

*However, more that 50% of small business fail in the first five years.* Someone has a passion for selling a particular item or they are an expert in a certain area and they attempt to create their own American Dream by launching their own business – and they trip over road blocks and pain points that make it impossible for them to succeed.

Many small business owners find themselves in a quandary of overwhelming issues that has them wandering around in a confusing cloud of details and contradictions. This 'overwhelm' of confusion means they cannot see clearly what path to follow to make their business a success.

***Defining the American Dream***

The first step in clearing up the confusion that can surround a business, is to clearly define what a business actually is – and according to Wikipedia, a business is "an organizational and legal entity made up of an association of people who share a common purpose and unite to focus their various talents and organize their collectively available skills or resources to achieve specific declared goals and are involved in the provision of goods and services to consumers."

If someone begins a business based on their expertise, say as an electrician, and they are the only employee, then they are self-employed, and they do not have a business. A business needs the leverage of employees to create an economic structure capable of returning a profit. When someone goes to work for themselves and simply trades their time for money, they have achieved self-employed status and have yet to create an actual business.

So, the self-employed person decides to create a business by establishing an office, hiring staff, purchasing equipment and launching full-tilt into an expanding enterprise. All too soon they are overwhelmed with confusing details, causing them to lose their clarity and their ability to make sound decisions, ultimately causing them to crash on the rocks of insolvency, usually after many months (or even years) of living with astronomically high levels of stress and a balance sheet that is in a downward spiral.

For them, the American Dream has turned into the American Nightmare. The good news is that it does not have to end this way!

The best way to make the American Dream come true is to get (and retain) crystal clear clarity on why you are in business, what is the focus of your business and what is your personal passion.

Creating a clear picture of what your business is supposed to be is the first step toward business success. I have a good friend who looks forward every fall to going out for cider, doughnuts and a quick run through the local corn maze. In an entertainment sense, it is fun to go down a blind alley, backtrack a few feet and then move on in a different direction and ultimately find your way out of the maze.

However, when you are in business and you feel like you are in a maze of confusion, this is when it stops being fun. When you are rushing down blind alleys trying to get the work done, keep clients happy, manage staff and keep revenue flowing, it is very hard to take the high view and determine what is the best path out of the maze.

Think about it in very practical terms. Something as simple as a corn maze can still be challenging when you are at ground level, walking down each path and having to take the time to figure out which way was out.

However, if you were able to climb a tree and look at the maze from a high vantage point, it would then become extremely easy to figure out the path through the maze. From the higher vantage point, you would have clarity on what route to take. Once you had the path memorized, you could then simply climb down from the tree, enter the maze, and very quickly find your way through to the other side.

***Creating the Picture on the Box***

We can also look at this from another point of view. Putting together a business can often feel like putting together a jigsaw puzzle, with the various sized pieces all jumbled together. Different people have different ways of putting together a puzzle. Some start by finding all the edge pieces, others sort by color or white space.

No matter what strategy someone uses to put together a puzzle, the most useful tool of all is to look at the picture on the box. This allows the person putting the jigsaw puzzle together to find a point of reference, and they can continue to look back at this picture as they put the puzzle together. This gives them the clarity they need to complete the puzzle.

However, business owners find themselves trying to put the puzzle of their business together without having the picture on the box for reference. They have no idea what the picture should look like, yet they are trying to put together a 1,000-piece puzzle!

In simple terms, for any business to be successful the owner needs to have extreme clarity on why they are in business, what business they are actually in and they need a well-oiled team in place to make the business function effortlessly.

Picture perfect success in business can only be attained if you have an accurate picture on your puzzle box of what your business should look like. Starting and operating a business without this clarity is a recipe for confusion.

### *The Expert Starts a Business*

"If your business depends on you, you don't own a business – you have a job. And, it's the worst job in the world because you are working for a lunatic!" Michael Gerber, author of the E-Myth

You might be the expert in what you do, but you might not be an expert in actually running a business. The first step towards clarity is admitting this – the next step is being very clear on what you are good at. It is important to know the difference between who we are and who we think we are and what other people expect us to be. If we think we can be all things to all people, we are setting ourselves up for failure and creating the environment that breeds confusion.

In his book the E-Myth, Michael Gerber outlines why most small businesses don't work. He outlines that business are run usually by one of three types of people: a "Technician", someone who knows how to do the technical work involved in a job, without much thought for the other, equally important roles described in the book of the "Entrepreneur" and the "Manager". These are not separate people, but distinct elements of our personalities. In other words, while we might be biased towards one, we all have elements of the other two, and to successfully run a small business, an owner must be able to be successful at all three aspects.

The Technician is someone who is an expert in his or her craft – like a hair dresser, baker or CPA. This often leads these people to go into business for themselves - they're good at what they do, and they know it, so why not reap the rewards of their labor instead of punching a timeclock for someone else? The Technician is happiest doing the work they are good at and ignoring the rest, which is, in the end, a total recipe for failure and a guarantee for creating chaos.

The Entrepreneur is the dreamer, the one who sets out to do something new, who reaches for the stars. The Entrepreneur lives in the future, thinking about what could be (rather than in the present). The Entrepreneur is often frustrated by how slow the world seems to move, and can jump ahead without having a foundation to stand on. They get excited by ideas and don't always know (or care) about the practical elements needed to bring the ideas into reality.

The Manager is the detail-oriented one, someone who dots the i's and crosses the t's, the one who remembers to pay the bills, and wants a well-organized world with no surprises; a world where things happen in an orderly, predictable manner.

Successful business owners need all three of these components: without the Entrepreneur, you might as well keep working for someone else as a Technician. Without any technical ability, the Entrepreneur must rely on others to get anything done, and without the organizational abilities of the Manager, the other two would probably find themselves with the electricity in the office turned off because they had other things to do than pay the bills.

That being said, it is also important to know that you CANNOT wear all the hats in a business and have it be successful. While you need to know and understand all three aspects, you CANNOT actually carry out all jobs within a business – there simply are not enough hours in a day.

### *Identifying the Confusion*

Alright, the expert has started a business and is now in a world of confusion – what next? Once they have realized they need to be equal parts Technician, Manager and Entrepreneur yet at the same time they cannot wear all the hats, the next step is taking an inventory of all the confusion. Or, putting it another way, what are your pain points?

In an article on SocializMonster.com, SEO expert Dagmar Gagtell outlines what she feels are the Top Ten pain points that cause mass confusion in business:

**1. Not enough money**

This is usually the top pain point for small businesses. All too often businesses are started on a "shoe string" and there is not enough money to support the business until it begins to be profitable. An example is a lawyer who opens a practice thinking they can charge $300 an hour and that should be plenty to live on – without stopping to consider that they need to employ staff, pay rent on an office etc. The rule of thumb is that it takes one to two years to break even and two to five years for a small business to turn a profit. This means you need to have access to money to invest in the startup stage in order to survive to the profit stage.

**2. Not enough hours in a day**

Many new business owners confuse getting their 'to-do' list done with having a workable strategy for running their business. They are so busy running around that they cannot manage their own or anyone else's time. They are always frazzled; the list never gets completed and the business never gets to the productive stage. There really are enough hours in a day, it just depends on how you spend them.

**3. Limited resources**

No, we are not talking about money again! Many business owners do not know where to go to get the assistance they need with basic things such as human resources, hiring expertise, knowledge of business tax structure and what the local zoning laws say about signs. The internet can provide many answers to questions, as can a business coach. Beware getting caught in the trap of thinking that you have to do it yourself because no one else can do it as well as you.

**4. Lack of business basics**
Starting and running a business is a science, not an art, and as such it can be learned. Remember when you were six and you wanted to learn how to ride a bike? That is when your parent stepped up and taught you how to do it. Yes, there were a few skinned knees and wobbly starts, but you learned how to do it. Be a 'lifelong learner'. Take classes, find a mentor, get a coach - and continually learn about how to make a business successful.

**5. Slow to adapt to changes in your industry**
The one true constant about today's business world is that the pace of change is always increasing. There are countless industries, businesses and jobs that existed 20 years ago that are no longer with us. Disruptive technology is happening all around us and your business has to keep pace with change or become extinct.

**6. Having a limiting beliefs mindset and/or negative attitude**
Many business owners 'buy' into what they are told about their own skill set. If you subconsciously (or consciously) believe that you are not a good manager, or that you are not good at customer service – then, guess what? Your belief makes it a fact! One of my favorite sayings is "The people who argue over whether the glass is half full or half empty miss the point that the glass can be refilled." No matter what your intensions are when you begin the day, negative things WILL happen. You can never control what happens TO you – you can only control how you react. Having a perpetual negative attitude only attracts more negativity – and guarantees that you will stay firmly mired in perpetual confusion. The good news is that all it takes is for you to decide that you are going to change your beliefs – then stand back and watch the magic happen!

**7. Life balance all out of whack**
Have you heard the expression that if you are in an airplane that experiences loss of pressure and the oxygen masks come down, you should put the mask over your own mouth first before you help others? Well, this holds true for business as well.

If you are so stressed out that you cannot work well with others, or your home life is a mess – how can you have the energy needed to make your business successful? You need to look after you first.

**8. Lack of appropriate support team**

Remember the definition of a business? The one where a single person is self-employed and NOT a business? However, the only thing worse than not having a support team is having the WRONG support team. Problems with staff can be the source of MAJOR confusion for a business owner! Whether you have the problem of unskilled, unreliable or just downright malicious staff, personnel problems can make or break a business. In fact, 23% of businesses that failed in 2015 cited not having the right team as the reason for the failure.

**9. No clarity of short or long-term goals**

What would happen if your drove down your driveway and turned left and just kept on driving? Would you end up in Phoenix, Arizona? The chances of that happening are pretty much zero – unless you select Phoenix as a destination, map out your route (using Rand McNally if you are over 50 or GPS if you are younger) and plan your trip. The funny thing is that many business owners take more time and care planning their vacations than they do planning for their business. Confusion will rein if you have no idea where you are going.

Or, on the flip side, you can suffer from what I call the LEAK syndrome. You know what your goal is, but you keep getting sidetracked by other things and leak into other areas. For example, if you are headed for Phoenix, you may decide to check out Seattle, WA – however, it's in the opposite direction!

**10. No specific purpose – The importance of knowing your why!**

Of course, making money is one of the reasons for going into business – we all need money to live on. However, if making money is the ONLY reason, you will find yourself covered in confusion and failing miserably.

Simon Sinek is a British/American author, speaker and marketing consultant who came to the attention of the business world when he launched his best seller "Start with Why" in 2009 followed by one of the most watched Ted Talks. Sinek says, "The goal is not to do business with everyone who needs what you have, the goal is to do business with people who believe what you believe." In order for that to be true, you need to know what you believe.

***Clarity is Up to You***

Clarity starts with you, the business owner. Clarity goes straight to the heart of why you are a business owner and what business you are in. Like money, business is a means to an end - it allows you to do what is important and purposeful in your life. Clarity allows your passion and your purpose to come together and provides a path to your highest and best life.

Talking about Picture Perfect clarity reminds me of the day my cousin and I were talking about my success on social media. She wanted to know how I got so many followers. I told her it was because I put "killer pictures" with my posts. However, I pronounced it 'pitcher'. She immediate pulled me up on that (she is a retired school teacher) and reminded me that the 'c' in picture was not silent. She gave me clarity on how to pronounce the word picture.

Clarity means that you will make easier and better decisions. Good decisions are made by following a process or framework and great decisions are a function of how clear the objective is – hence the need for clarity. Lack of clarity breeds muddled decisions.

With clarity, you can leverage internal and external resources empowering others to act, innovate, and offer solutions that support the vision and goals of your business. The ultimate result is exponential growth in organizational power (the ability to do work, solve problems, and move toward the vision or goal).

Clarity reduces conflict and stress which improves efficiency. Typically, there is always more work than there are resources. Conflicts arise and requires intervention (management) to resolve. Clarity provides the basis of a self-governing process that reduces conflict.

The process of creating clarity greatly enhances your ability to find and retain the right people. Having the right diversity of people has proven to be more important to success than an idea. People who are inclined with the same values and purpose will be attracted to your company – but only if you have the clarity of what your purpose actually is!

Defining what you want the future of your business to look like is not easy. Working on clarity forces you to reflect and really understand what is important to you personally and to your business. You have to 'put it out there' and then be ready to be held accountable.

Join me for the journey as we go through the rest of this book, which will give you a road map of how you can create clarity about yourself and about your business and create the perfect picture on your puzzle box, giving you the guide you need to go from confusion to clarity in your business.

# Chapter Two

## Defining your Passion and Getting to Your "Why"

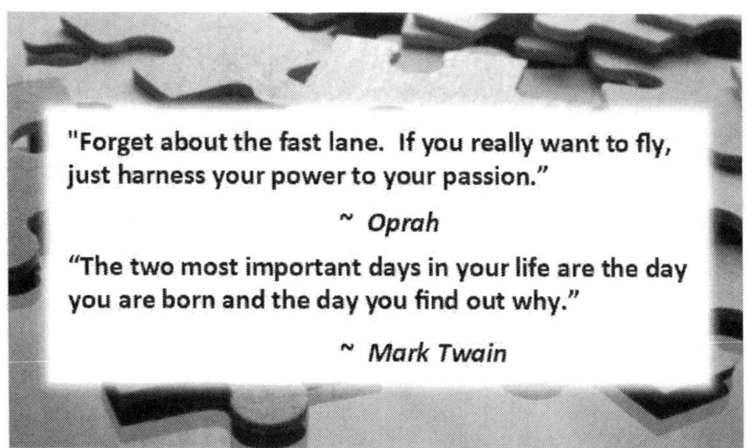

"Forget about the fast lane. If you really want to fly, just harness your power to your passion."
~ Oprah
"The two most important days in your life are the day you are born and the day you find out why."
~ Mark Twain

Mark Twain said that the definition of success was making your vocation your vacation. According to him, when you reached that stage you would 'never work another day in your life' because you enjoyed your work so much.

The first step in gaining clarity and creating the 'picture on the box' depicting your perfect business, is clearly defining 'what is your why'. What makes you want to get up in the morning? What would you do even if you did not get paid?

Sometimes looking back in time can give you a good perspective on things in the present. In 1987, Marsha Sinetar wrote a book entitled "Do What You Love and The Money Will Follow." In the first chapter she outlines what many of us know – a large percentage of Americans are working at jobs that they hate. They view their jobs as merely a 'means to an end' of providing for themselves and their families.

Sinetar points out how this is a tragedy, as our working life composes the majority of our overall life. She goes on to outline how enhancing our self-esteem is the first step toward finding our passion. "The world is as we are - an old Hindu saying. As we enhance our self-esteem, so we enhance our working lives."

As I pointed out in Chapter 1, Simon Sinek is a British/American author, speaker and marketing consultant who came to the attention of the business world when he launched his best seller "Start with Why" in 2009. His book starts with a comparison of the two main ways to influence human behavior: manipulation and inspiration. Sinek argues that inspiration is the more powerful and sustainable of the two. He says that people are inspired by a sense of purpose (or "Why"), and that this should come first, before How and What.

He followed up on this concept in 2017 when he published Find Your Why: A Practical Guide for Discovering Purpose for You and Your Team in tandem with David Mean and Peter Cocker. This practical guide gives readers a workshop approach to helping them identify their WHY.

Finding your WHY usually begins with discovering what you are passionate about and then finding a practical way to utilize that in your business. When you Google "discover your passion" a whole list of conflicting articles and ideas spring on to the screen.

Rebecca Burn-Callander, former Enterprise Editor for The Telegraph, wrote a New Year's blog on finding your passion. She writes, "Finding your passion could be easier than you think. By answering these questions honestly, you could work out what to do with the rest of your life."

"What subject could I read 500 books about without getting bored?"

"What could I do for five years straight without getting paid?"

"What would I spend my time doing if I had complete financial abundance to do anything?"

Other pundits say that you have to find your passion with your heart and not your mind, that taking interest inventories or passion quizzes is not the way to find what makes you want to get up in the morning.

As with all good stories, no matter how thin you slice it there are always two sides. Everyone is at a different point in their lives and they will need different types of assistance in figuring out what they want to do when they grow up!

### *Finding My WHY*

It feels like I have always been in a business environment. I learned my soft skills years ago from some older seasoned colleagues while working in a family owned flower shop in Pennsylvania.

I learned about the importance of creating a great customer experience and how communication was a key ingredient when building long term relationships. And, of course, I learned the obvious – that people buy from people and businesses they know, like and trust.

My father was a banker and my mother was a bookkeeper, so the financial services path seemed the best way to achieve success. I graduated from King's College and went to work for Deloitte & Touché and then Marquis & Associates.

At the tender age of 29, I became a partner in an insurance agency. We specialized in providing insurance and surety bonds for major construction sites all over New Jersey. I was the CFO of the agency, wore many hats and was involved in implementing cost effective agency management systems, which means I had to really study and understand every aspect of the business.

All of my hard work paid off, when the agency was acquired by industry giant Willis in 1997 and I was the liaison between my company and Willis during the merger. I continued to work for Willis, and in 2003, I transferred to the New York division of the company when they made me the Regional Finance Officer and I assumed responsibility for a $100 million market region.

In 2010, Willis acquired another agency and asked me to integrate the various personal lines of insurance into the main company. This was a feather in my cap, to have such a large company acknowledge what I brought to the table in my capacity as CFO.

In 2012 I decided it was time to strike out on my own and I founded Hatrak Associates, LLC. I was originally helping professionals in transition get clarity on what they wanted and assisting them in branding themselves on social media as a way to create a path to their next job.

## Picture Perfect Business Success

My light bulb moment came when a person I had helped sent me a hand-written thank-you note that spoke of my gift as a coach. This got me thinking about my background in Accounting, my experience in business and how this could be combined with my newly found passion for helping people.

This helped me quantify what my passion was (helping people) and all of my other experiences made the practical application simple – take what I knew about the financial and business worlds and coach small business owners (particularly in the financial and professional services space) in how to be awesome. I decided to use the Brian Tracy franchise of Focal Point Coaching to fast track my coaching business.

Being a business coach has now become my last stop on my own personal professional train because everything I have done in my career has led me to where I am now and where I want to go in the future. I really enjoy helping people create their definition of success and then help them find the clarity needed to define their 'why' and reach their ultimate goal.

I can hear the muttering now about how many coaches there are out there at the moment. However, many coaches come from the academic world. I come from the real world of hard knocks. I was a business owner and I built and sold a business. I have worked for large and small companies. I have helped a lot of people brand themselves and become sustainable, and I maintain my license as a CPA in Pennsylvania and a New Jersey producers license for Property, Casualty, Health and Personal insurance lines. (Which means I keep up with continuing education for many of the types of businesses that I coach.)

I have found my why – and it is the passion for making a difference by helping people create their picture-perfect business. However, the search for clarity does not stop with just one "aha" moment.

I continued to educate myself on who was in this space and what they were saying – I realized I needed to 'keep up' and always be prepared to give my clients the best possible mix of education and advice.

I am the CPA that doesn't talk about numbers. I help business owners identify gaps in their business and provide tools to fill the gaps faster than they could if left to their own devices. One of the tools I am passionate about and use is a Behavior Analysis called DiSC® - it is simple to learn and understand. It measures your most comfortable behaviors or how you naturally prefer to do things. It is a basic and user-friendly theory of human behavior that gives people a common language to better understand themselves and others.

I had a major 'aha' moment when I discovered this behavior assessment, as it made the concept of communication and how it influences behavior crystal clear. If you're communicating and selling the same way to everyone, you're doing it incorrectly, because everyone has a different behavior style. People buy from people they know, like and trust. So, the quicker people know, like and trust you, the easier it is for you to become profitable and sustainable.

By combining my knowledge, skills and experience with my passion for helping people I have been able to build a successful coaching business. I hop out of bed each morning with the realization that I have the luxury of having my "vocation be my vacation."

To quote Simon Sinek, "It is one of life's greatest joys to wake up in the morning... every morning, with a clear sense of why that day matters, why every day matters. This is what it means to find your WHY. This is the start of an inspiring journey... your inspiring journey."

I always tell my clients that they will make more waves in their pond if their clients believe that they are the best person to help them define and achieve success on their terms.

That's my WHY!

My purpose is to help business owners define and achieve success on their terms. And in many cases, I help them do it faster than they could on their own. And HOW do I do that?

I involve them in the process 100%. I begin every workshop with my favorite quote from Benjamin Franklin... Tell me and I forget, Teach Me and I remember, Involve me and I learn. I have learned that my passion is to help people – by coaching them into being better business owners!

***Practical Passion Steps***

So, how do you find your passion? Do you just take an online interest inventory, or do you simply list all your favorite things to do?

One very good place to begin is to sit down with a blank sheet of paper and describe in detail your ideal day. What would you be doing and where would you be doing it? How would you feel and who would you be interacting with? This exercise can give you some valuable insights on what you enjoy.

There are also several online "passion tests" that can shed some light on the matter. However, one of the simplest ways is to simply remember what you are good at and what you enjoy doing. Or, what you would do even if you were not paid? What would you do simply for the love of doing it?

A friend of mine shared a story of how she found her passion in life. After many years in business, mostly in the marketing space, she came to a point in her life where just simply working for money or owning a business was not enough. She started a non-profit working with young people to teach them about business. She found that working with the young people individually and in groups was sheer fun and she was able to share all the expertise she had gathered while working for corporations and for herself.

Benjamin Disraeli, a 19th century British Prime Minister, once said, "Man is only great when he acts from passion." Today's aspiring entrepreneur, exploring avenues of creativity to find your passion is likely the quickest route to increase your chances of having a successful business.

**Help in Defining Your Passion**
Try the following exercises to see if you can pinpoint your passions in business.

**Exercise 1 – Revisit your childhood – what did you enjoy doing?**
"It's amazing how disconnected we become to the things that brought us the most joy in favor of what's practical," says Rob Levit, an Annapolis based creativity expert, speaker and business consultant.

Levit suggests making a list of all the things you remember enjoying as a child and then assessing if you enjoy that activity now. For example, Frank Lloyd Wright, America's greatest architect, played with wooden blocks all through childhood and perhaps well past it. This provided the testing ground for his ultimate career as an architect.

"Research shows that there is much to be discovered in play, even as adults," Levit says. Revisit some of the positive activities, foods and events of childhood and see how they can be translated and added into your life at the present moment. How can those past experiences shape your business choices now?

**Exercise 2 – Make a Creativity/Vision Board**
Start by taking a large poster board, put the words "New Business" in the center and create a collage of images, sayings, articles, poems and other inspirations, suggests Michael Michalko, a creativity expert based in Rochester, N.Y. He is the author of creativity books and tools, including ThinkPak.

"The idea behind this is that when you surround yourself with images of your intention - who you want to become or what you want to create - your awareness and passion will grow," Michalko says.

As your vision board evolves and becomes more focused, you will begin to recognize what is missing and imagine ways to fill the blanks and realize your vision. There is much evidence that shows that visualizing what you want in very specific terms is the first step toward achieving it.

**Exercise 3 – Identify People Who are Where You Want to be**
Remember, you don't have to reinvent the wheel. Study people who have been successful in the area you want to pursue.

For example, during the recession, many people shied away from the real estate market because they thought it was a dead end. However, that can be the perfect time to jump in to a business - when most others are bailing out - because no matter the business, there are people who are successful in it. Study them, figure out how and why they were able to remain successful when everyone else is folding their tents and leaving and then set up structures to follow their lead.

"If you want to be creative, create a rigorous and formal plan," Levit says. "It's not the plan that is creative; it's the process that you go through that opens up so many possibilities."

**Exercise 4 – Start Doing What you Love – then Write the Business Plan**

A lot of people wait until they have an extensive business plan written down, along with angel investors wanting to throw cash at them - and their ideas never see the light of day, according to Cath Duncan, a Calgary, Canada-based creativity expert and life coach who works with entrepreneurs and other professionals.

She recommends doing what you enjoy - even if you haven't yet figured out how to monetize it. Test what it might be like to work in an area you're passionate about, build your business network and ask for feedback that will help you develop and refine a business plan.

It's a way to not only show the value you would bring, but you can also get testimonials that will help launch your business when you're ready to make it official and begin the journey to becoming an entrepreneur.

**Exercise 5 – Take a Break from Only Focusing on Business**

While it might feel uncomfortable to step outside of business mode, the mind sometimes needs a rest from such bottom-line thinking. Maybe for you, it will be creative writing, painting, running or even collecting something obscure.

After you take a mental vacation indulging in something you're passionate about come back to your desk and write down any business ideas that come to mind. You will find that you have a different perspective because you too a break to appreciate the wonder in the world.

**Exercise 6 - Powerful Questions to Uncover Your Purpose**

For each of the prompts below, write for a minimum of five minutes. Don't censor yourself. Write freely. Jot down whatever comes to mind, no matter how silly it seems.

- Name the top 3 peak experiences in your life. What do they have in common? What does this tell you about yourself?
- If money weren't a problem, what would you spend your day doing?
- What dreams have you given up on? Why? Did fear play a role? Did your values change? How can you rekindle forgotten interests?
- What is the hardest thing you have ever had to overcome? How did this influence you?
- What activity are you doing when it feels like time flies by?

These powerful questions can help you strip away limiting beliefs to find your true calling and work you find deeply meaningful. That doesn't mean it'll be easy, but it will be rewarding.

At the end of the day, introspection isn't enough. You have to take consistent action to make your dreams a reality. But when you take the time to look inward, you may be surprised by what you find. Your passion might have been waiting there all along, just waiting for you to notice and to light the spark.

### *Be Passionate with a Purpose*

While discovering your passion and your WHY are an important step in gaining clarity about your business, for it to 'fly' in the practical world you need to distill it down into a specific 'purpose statement'.

Many companies today have a mission statement which drives HOW you follow a path and a vision statement which describes WHAT is the destination or goal. But how many businesses have a purpose statement? A Purpose Statement captures succinctly WHY the organization exists and WHAT it does. And what about you as a professional? Do you have a purpose statement? Do you know your Why?

**Purpose Statement Planning Worksheet (Finding Your Why)**

1. Why does our business exist?
2. Why was the business founded? What was its original purpose?
3. In the future, will our purpose change? (if yes, then how)
4. What specifically, will we spend our time doing? Not, what will our people do, but what will we do?
5. How will we know if we have accomplished it? How will we measure ourselves?
6. What constraints of time will we place on accomplishing our purpose?
7. How will our entire organization be compelled to participate?

**Draft Purpose Statement**
**Instructions:**
Taking into consideration your thoughts, what is the essential purpose of the organization?

Boil it down to a single sentence that is simple and memorable. (Fifteen words or less)

WHAT IS THE PURPOSE OF OUR ORGANIZATION?
Your Purpose Statement (Defining Your Why)
TO_____________SO THAT_____________
Example:
To: Create an HR Consulting Firm (the contribution that you make)
SO THAT: Small businesses will be able to comply with HR law. (the impact on others)

Qualities of a Purpose Statement

S Specific - Unique to your organization.

M Measurable - How will you know it has been accomplished?

A Attainable - Achievable within the realm of faith.

R Relevant - Worthy of accomplishment.

T Time-bound - Incorporates a time frame for accomplishment.

S Strategic - It will capture the resources of our entire organization.

### *Pulling it All Together*

Discovering your passion and putting it into practical terms is the best way to begin creating the clarity needed to ensure your business is successful. At the risk of repeating myself, as Simon Sinek says, "The goal is not to do business with everyone who needs what you have, the goal is to do business with people who believe what you believe." In order for that to be true, you need to know what you believe!

The Simon Sinek team summed it up perfectly in the book "Find Your Why". "Once you understand your WHY, you'll be able to clearly articulate what makes you feel fulfilled and to better understand what drives your behavior when you're at your natural best. When you can do that, you'll have a point of reference for everything you do going forward. You'll be able to make more intentional choices for your business, your career and your life. . . From now on, you'll start with WHY."

# Section Two

## Vision - What is Your Ultimate Goal?

# Chapter Three

## Creating the Picture on the Box

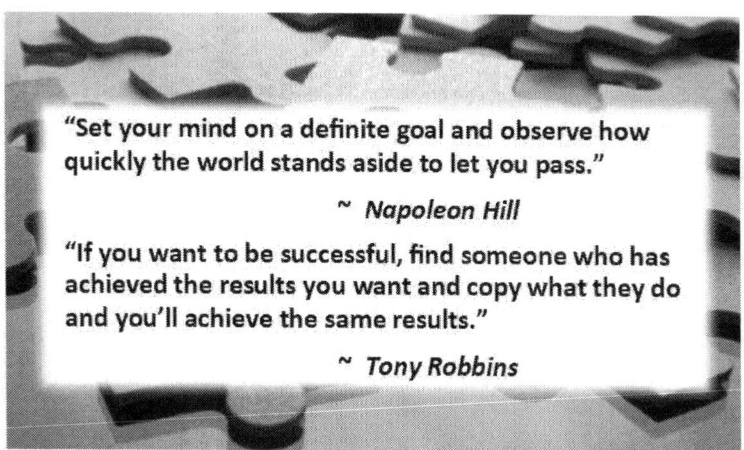

"Set your mind on a definite goal and observe how quickly the world stands aside to let you pass."
~ Napoleon Hill
"If you want to be successful, find someone who has achieved the results you want and copy what they do and you'll achieve the same results."
~ Tony Robbins

Putting together a business is much like putting together a puzzle. That brings us to the question, what is the most important piece of a jigsaw puzzle? Some say the corner, some say the edges, but in reality, the most important piece of a puzzle is the picture on the box.

That is your starting point with figuring out how to put all the pieces together, and it is what you reference all the way through until you have the puzzle completed.

Have you ever tried to complete a 1,000 piece puzzle without knowing what the picture is? No, that doesn't happen, because the puzzle comes in a box with the picture right on the front. The same logic applies when it comes to your business. If you have no clue what you want your business to look like, how can you ever be successful?

The infamous Cheshire Cat, who appears in Alice in Wonderland, gave us a true window on wisdom when he said, "If you don't know where you are going, any road will get you there." It is also like my analogy in a previous chapter – if you leave your driveway and turn right and just keep driving, chances are you will never end up in Phoenix, Arizona!

The only way to get there is to decide that is your ultimate destination, use a map or your GPS to plot a course, and begin to travel toward Phoenix, checking each day back against your travel plan to ensure you are making progress in the right direction.

So, how do you go about creating the picture on the box and plotting your course? The first step is to figure out where you are right now.

### *Sigmoid Curve*

Everything in life is complex, and business is no exception. However, there are mathematical ways to represent complex ideas that make them easier to understand. One such math construct is the Sigmoid Curve, a useful way to explain the lifecycle of a business.

The Sigmoid Curve is essentially a representation of time (the horizontal axis) and activity (vertical axis).

The magic of this concept is that is can be applied to just about any situation and set of events.

More things in the human experience go through these phases, from the rise and fall of nations to the rise and fall of technology.

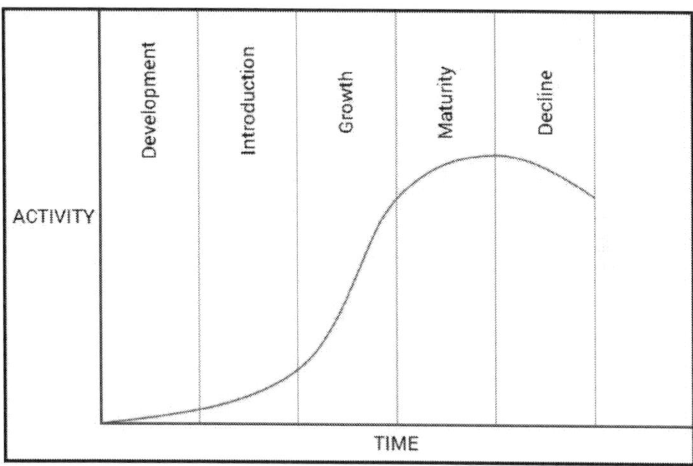


In **Phase One, the Learning Phase**, which covers Development and Introduction, you will be extraordinarily busy, facing challenges and difficulties, learning and trying new things as you scramble to make your business successful. This is the phase where many new companies never make it beyond the initial startup into the growth phase. They stumble and fall and then they do not have the financial resources or the will to survive. This accounts for the high rate of failure of startup businesses.

In the **Growth and Maturity phase**, you will find yourself as an owner experiencing a state of high energy and even exhilaration, as your business and sales grow exponentially. New ideas and new possibilities are cropping up on all sides, and your success is breeding even more success! In this phase some mistakes are made, but they usually are just learning experiences that lead to further success.

However, without appropriate adjustments, the third and final phase of **Decline** is inevitable. This concept is very helpful when applied to business.

The trick is to identify where you are on the curve at a particular point in time, where do you want to be in 1 year, 2 years, 5 years and so on.

The second trick it to identify when to hop off the current curve and move on to something else before reaching the downward decline. The secret to constant growth as a business is being able to identify when you reach that point – if you miss it, then it is hard to identify a new curve and have the resources to transfer to it before bottoming out in the decline phase.

***Where Are You Now?***

GPS (short for Global Position System) is fast becoming part of our everyday lives. However, GPS is useless if it does not have a starting point. In order for the system to work and tell you how to navigate to your destination, the system must know exactly where you are on the map at your starting point.

It is the same in business. In order to determine where you are going, you must first determine where you are now. Ok, once you know where you are, you can then begin to formulate what the ultimate goal is for your business. You need to paint the picture of your future, so you can then put the puzzle together to match the picture.

Why is this important? Because everything begins in the mind. If you don't define what success is for you, how can you ever know if you have achieved it?

Let me share an excerpt from one of my favorite books, "Think and Grow Rich" by Napoleon Hill.

> "I imagine some readers will question the statement that a mere, intangible DESIRE can be converted into its physical equivalent. Doubtless some will say, "You cannot convert NOTHING into SOMETHING!" The answer is in the story of United States Steel. That giant organization was created in the mind of one man (Charles M. Schwab). The plan by which the organization was provided with the steel mills that gave it financial stability was created in the mind of the same man. His FAITH, his DESIRE, his IMAGINATION, his PERSISTENCE were the real ingredients that went into United States Steel. The steel mills and mechanical equipment acquired by the corporation, AFTER IT HAD BEEN BROUGHT INTO LEGAL EXISTENCE, were incidental, but careful analysis will disclose the fact that the appraised value of the properties acquired by the corporation increased in value by an estimated SIX HUNDRED MILLION DOLLARS, by the mere transaction which consolidated them under one management."

In other words, Charles M. Schwab's IDEA, plus the FAITH with which he conveyed it to the minds of J. P. Morgan and the others, was marketed for a profit of approximately $600,000,000. Not an insignificant sum for a single IDEA!.... RICHES begin in the form of THOUGHT!

### *Clear Picture Leads to Reality*

Many people have heard of The Secret. The book and video burst onto the scene in 2006 from Australian author and film maker Rhonda Byrne. The key message of The Secret is that everyone has the ability to create their own reality. In other words, "thoughts can become things and you can manifest what you concentrate on." This best-selling, self-help guide by Rhonda Byrne, is available in 50 different languages. It received critical acclaim for the way it offers straightforward techniques to transform your life.

Byrne and the other makers of The Secret Documentary interviewed the world's best-known Law of Attraction teachers to produce (in lay person's terms) a definition of what this Law is and how to apply it to your life.

Some of the most famous experts interviewed included Jack Canfield, Bob Proctor, Joe Vitale and John Assaruf. Some of the experts specialized in metaphysics or the quantum physics of the Law of Attraction, while others are leading authorities in psychology or personal development.

All of the speakers discussed how desires can shape the world and they explored how to cultivate the thought processes that would support manifestation. The documentary became a global phenomenon. Viewers reported the many exciting ways in which positive thinking helped to improve their lives.

To date, the book has sold more than 20 million copies. It continues to attract attention for its accessible, empowering style. As in the documentary, The Secret book covers simple ways of explaining using the Law of Attraction.

According to the Secret, The Law of Attraction is for everyone, and it's working all the time. You don't need a specialist skillset to use it. You just need to develop more refined, positive goals and focus on rooting out negativity in your life.

### *Creating the Picture on the Box*

Your vision and mission statements form the core of your business plan. Anyone who reads through your vision and mission statements will know what your business does, how you help people, where you're going, and how you plan to get there.

Right now, we are concentrating on your vision statement (we are creating the picture on the box). Your vision statement needs to be all about looking ahead and what your destination looks like – and, of course, how will you know when you have arrived.

Your mission statement is all about 'doing', and your day-to-day operations that provides the steps that move you toward your vision. (We will discuss more about this in chapter 5)

Do you ever stop to think about what it is that YOU really want in life? I'm not talking about that new car or that dream vacation to a far way place – I'm talking about what kind of life you want to create, the one that will have your springing out of bed every day, ready to hit the ground running and you are filled with purpose and joy. The life that is not only meaningful, but exciting – the life that is perfect for you in every way.

I'm talking about the kind of life where you wake up filled with joy and purpose. The kind of life where you're doing work that's meaningful and exciting. The kind of life that is perfectly "you" in every way.

So, to begin painting the picture on your puzzle box you need to have a clear idea of what you like, what you enjoy and where you are ultimately going with your life, both personally and professionally. We tend to look at business icons like Richard Branson (who seem to have everything) and think that they are special or lucky and we cannot have the life that they have.

Do you want to know the number one road block to creating the life of your dreams? *The number one roadblock is not knowing exactly what you want!* There are millions of choices and countless paths down which we can travel. For example, you may say you wish you had more money, but if you do not have a clear plan on how much money you want and how you are going to get it, it will remain only a wish instead of a concrete goal. (Remember, goals are wishes with deadlines.)

So, creating the picture on the box is the first, best and most important step for you to be able to build the picture-perfect business.

***Step by Step***

If creating the ultimate vision for your business seems overwhelming to define, just remember that there is only one way to eat an elephant – one bite at a time! Let's take this slow and easy.

One way to approach mapping out your vision statement is to begin with a basic exercise. Simply define your ideal day. How do you do that? Begin by asking yourself a few basic questions.

- What time do I want to wake up?
- What is the first thing that I do?
- How do I feel?
- Who do I hang out with?
- What is my passion for work?
- What is my passion for my personal life?
- Where am I living?
- Who am I living with?
- How do I spend my mornings?
- How do I spend my afternoons?
- How do I spend my evenings?
- And, the most telling question of all - What do I ultimately want out of life?

Another way to approach defining your ideal day is to think back over your life and select two to three days where you were really happy and really fulfilled – and simply describe those days in detail. Then, analyze the details and determine how you can create more of those days.

### *Crafting the Vision*

Alright, now that you have defined what you want your life and your business to look like, it is time to quantify everything into a vision statement (the picture on the box).

This is a word picture of what you want your future business to look like and it can be a few sentences or a few paragraphs long. Just keep in mind that this is the overview, not the day to day implementation plan.

Your vision statement should be clear, concise and to the point – and it should have significant meaning for you as it will outline how you help people, what value you offer to them and how to will deliver your value.

It outlines how you help people, the value you offer to the world, and what you plan to achieve as a business.

A Vision Statement is:

- Aspirational, in that is it about your goals for the future
- Inspirational, as it provides meaning and direction for your day to day work
- Motivational, as it will provide a reason for you and your staff for the work that you do.

Your vision statement should have your business values, business goals, strengths and opportunities clearly defined. It is in essence your business story, a clear definition of why your business exists.

## Implementation - Make a Vision Board

A fun and engaging way to begin crafting your vision statement is to begin with a vision board. You can do this with pictures and clearly written answers to some of the following questions:

- Who does your business help?
- What's the purpose of your business?
- How do you want to make the world a better place with your business?
- What problems does your business solve?
- What's your ultimate aim for your business?

Have fun with this, collect picture, inspirational sayings – anything that speaks to your ultimate purpose.

## Presenting the Picture on the Box

Now that you have defined your ideal day, clearly defined the purpose of your business and your audience and have collected pictures depicting various aspects of your vision, it's time to create the picture on the box.

The first step is to create the skeleton of your vision statement. Use short words and sentences, make it fun and engaging yet crystal clear in terms of meaning. Focus on what your business does for others, how you help your customers and inspire your employees. Remember, shorter is better! Get to the point and make sure it is clear, even if the person reading it has never met you.

Be sure and ask for feedback, to ensure that you have used the clearest language possible and that a variety of people understand what you mean.

Once the vision statement is complete, then have fun putting together a vision board, with pictures, inspirational saying and the final copy of your vision statement. You now have completed the picture on the box and you now have the clarity you need to begin putting together the puzzle of your successful business.

In his book, A brief guide to world domination (How to Live a Remarkable Life in a Conventional World), Chris Guillebeau tells the story of Leo Babauta. In 2005, Leo Babauta was in a bad place: he was overweight, in debt, a smoker, and a procrastinator. He felt stuck and he didn't know how to change his habits.

Then he discovered some invaluable advice to help him overcome his rut and change his habits for the long-term. He quit smoking and started running. He ran a marathon. He began waking up earlier and eating healthier. And then he started to share his learnings and experiences on his blog, *Zen Habits*. He had a focus on creating and posting quality content on a regular basis and people began to respond.

By the end of 2007, he had 26,000 readers, had sold a book deal, had got out of debt, and quit his day job – all because he decided to concentrate on the positive. All because he had made it a priority to see how he could help other people recreate the success he had created, he now has over 240,000 subscribers and a thriving blogging and writing business that provides meaningful value to his clients.

# Chapter Four

## Getting Set For the Journey

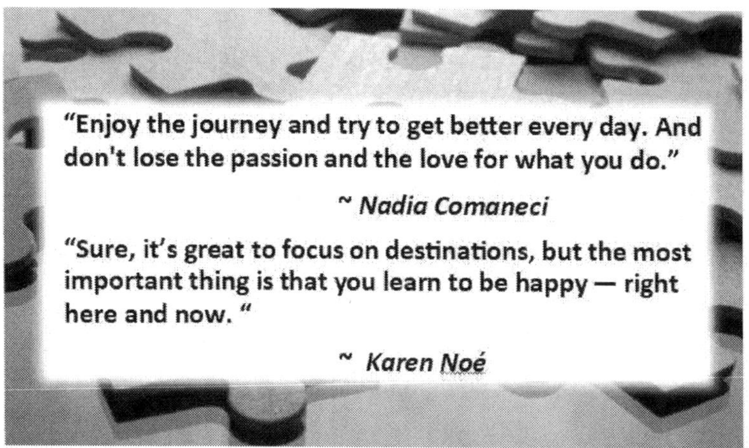

"Enjoy the journey and try to get better every day. And don't lose the passion and the love for what you do."
~ Nadia Comaneci
"Sure, it's great to focus on destinations, but the most important thing is that you learn to be happy — right here and now. "
~ Karen Noé

When the picture on your box is complete, it is now time to begin the journey of putting together the puzzle. However, before we begin on the specifics, let's talk about the journey. It is important to figure out how to enjoy the ride, so don't think you have to arrive at your destination before you can then love what you do.

Always keep things in perspective and realize that every day has a purpose, you should find joy in the small things and realize small things lead to big results. The first pieces of the puzzle that you should be putting together are self-care and life balance.

***Taking Care of You***

Jayson DeMers, founder of SEO company Audience Bloom and a regular contributor to the website Entrepreneur.com, came up with the following list. The list is based on what lessons business owners learned as they began their businesses, and gradually attained leadership, decision making, and adaptability skills needed to get ahead. This list represents the top 50 things they did.

**1. Read books. Fiction, nonfiction:** As long as you're reading, you're getting new perspectives and expanding your mind. Remember, your mind is a muscle and it needs to be exercised to stay healthy.

**2. Read the news.** Keep an eye on what's going on in your industry and in the world at large. Knowledge is priceless. However, do not get bogged down in the negative news.

**3. Attend industry conferences.** Get to know who your colleagues are and stay up to date on the latest developments and resources available to your business. Who knows, you might even find a mentor.

**4. Watch your competitors.** If they launch a new product, you're the first one who should know about it. Figure out how it might impact your business, and can you do something even better?

**5. Create new rules** for yourself. Set new limitations, such as allowing shorter periods for distraction, or making yourself do and try new things.

**6. Learn new technologies.** Technology can improve almost any process, so stay attuned to any new products on the horizon. How can they help you? How can they help your business?

**7. Engage in personal hobbies.** Passion is at the core of every influential entrepreneur's life. Find enjoyable, stimulating hobbies to help bring yours out (and, no, work does not count as a hobby).

**8. Talk to strangers.** You never know whom you might meet - a new partner? A mentor? An investor? An employee? Cultivate the art of being able to start a conversation with a stop sign! Be curious, be empathetic, be a good listening – you never know when you will hear a million-dollar idea.

**9. Network professionally.** The same goes for professional networking events, though here you'll also have a chance to build your own reputation. However, don't be the 'used car sales' type by being too pushy. Just let others know how you can help them.

**10. Give back to the community.** Volunteer, if you have time. You'll meet new people and make your community a better place and you'll sleep better at night knowing that you have made a difference.

**11. Make yourself available to your team.** Every day, make yourself accessible for questions, concerns and conversation. The time and effort you put into developing them will come back 10-fold to you as a business owner.

**12. Minimize your decisions.** Don't waste time on small decisions. Focus on the big ones. Look at all the angles and then take the leap. Nothing will happen if you don't make decisions.

**13. Find ways to improve everything.** Look at everything with a critical eye, and always see the potential for improvement – then be committed to making the improvements happen.

**14. Meditate.** It will give you clarity of mind, reduce your stress and make you more focused. And, it will help you control the 'monkey mind' of too much worry.

**15. Sleep well.** Eight hours of sleep will make you healthier, physically and mentally. Make a mandatory bedtime a priority.

**16. Eat healthy.** Complex carbohydrates, proteins and healthy fats are brain foods that keep you going. Plan ahead and make sure you have what you need when you need it – reaching for junk food is the first instinct when driven only by hunger.

**17. Exercise physically**. A healthy body makes a healthy mind. Even if it's just doing floor exercises and jumping jacks in the office.

**18. Exercise mentally**. Improve your critical thinking, focus and memory, with games and puzzles.

**19. SWOT analyze everything.** See the Strengths, Weaknesses, Opportunities and Threats in everything.

**20. Go the extra mile.** Overachieve at even the smallest of life's activities. Under promise and over deliver.

**21. Adapt.** Get used to changing your plans on a whim and rolling with the punches. Nothing in life is cast in concrete. And remember, the rigid trees are the ones that get knocked down in a storm – the supple ones who bend with the wind are the ones that survive.

**22. Continue your education.** Make it a point to learn something new every day. What you learn will help your business and make you a more interesting person.

**23. Invest inwardly.** Spend time improving yourself. The successful business person reads over 60 books each year – how many have you read so far this year?

**24. Try new things.** You never know where you'll get your next flash of inspiration. New experiences will open up new pathways in your brain, making anything possible!

**25. Start small.** Whenever you try something new, start out small and slow - you can always scale up – but it is very hard to scale down.

**26. Reward hard work.** Take time to express gratitude to those who deserve it. A smile and a thank you go a long way.

**27. Weed out negativity.** Nip poor attitudes and negativity in the bud whenever you see them – and make sure you are not the source of the negativity.

**28. Relieve group stress.** Stress is contagious, so do what you can to lower it in the office. A smile, a well placed joke, a lunch 'on the house' – it's the little things that count.

**29. Find new passions.** Again, passion is key to achieving success as an entrepreneur. Find yours in as many places as possible, not just at the office. New passions create excitement, excitement leads to new ideas and they can lead just about anywhere.

**30. Focus on customer perspectives.** Your customers are what keep your business going, so you need to prioritize their needs above everything else.

**31. Run the numbers.** Learn to see everything in terms of its objective value. Never let emotions get in the way of reading the numbers.

**32. Stay calm.** No matter how bad or hectic things get, you need to be the calmest one in the group. Avoid the 'chicken little' syndrome of running around saying the sky is falling.

**33. Give feedback.** People need an honest assessment of how they are doing.

**34. Listen to feedback.** Accept that you aren't perfect, and listen to how you can do better. If you are going to give feedback you need to able to accept it as well.

**35. Remain humble.** Don't let your ego take over your personality. No one likes a know it all.

**36. Form new partnerships.** There's always an opportunity for mutual benefit among professionals. This can create mutually beneficial leverage.

**37. Work with mentors.** Talk to people more experienced than you are, and listen to what they have to say, and be willing to implement changes.

**38. Trust your instincts.** Data is useful, but it can take you only so far. Don't ignore your instincts. If your gut is telling you that something is wrong, run away.

**39. Practice patience.** Remember, Rome was not built in a day and neither will your business.

**40. Accept challenges.** Tell yourself that it is ok to take calculated risks.

**41. Experiment with new routines.** Try doing your work in new and different ways. Something that simple can get your brain to travel down new pathways and the end results can be quite spectacular.

**42. Stay frugal.** Don't spend time or money on something unless it's truly valuable to you or your business. Just because you had a good month does not mean to can buy the $600 purse or $1,000 shoes.

**43. Have hard conversations.** Don't let fears or anxieties hold you back from saying what needs to be said – to yourself, your staff or your clients.

**44. Live your brand.** Incorporate your brand values into your daily life.

**45. Refrain from personal judgment.** When people make mistakes, don't hold it against them. Point out the issues and help them learn.

**46. Maintain an ideal atmosphere.** Inject your surroundings with personality and life, from your office to your car to your bedroom. Every room you walk into should be enticing to you.

**47. Eliminate chronic distractions.** If something is preventing you from working or achieving something, get rid of it. Remember, Facebook will NOT vanish if you don't check it every five minutes.

**48. Automate what you can.** Reduce manual actions through delegation and technology whenever possible – don't waste your talents on drudgery.

**49. Forget the idea of perfection.** You'll never be perfect, so forget about even trying. Instead, focus on continually striving to be better.

**50. Make personal time.** Maintain sanity by always making an oasis in your day for yourself.

Even with these habits in tow, there's no such thing as a perfect entrepreneur, and no entrepreneur becomes successful overnight. Stick with these habits and prioritize your own development. No matter what, you'll make progress and get closer to your goals.

Most small business owners suffer from constantly being in "overdrive," always working at a pace that makes mere mortals seem slow by comparison. And while a fast pace can aid small business owners in getting ahead of the competition, it can also lead to burnout, and you can't compete when you are a husk of your former self.

For years, many have sought to achieve the seemingly mythical ideal of "work-life balance." While many experts say it's simply not possible, the truth is that defining one's work-life balance is really in the eye of the beholder.

### *What Is Work-Life Balance?*

Wikipedia defines it as : "Work–life balance is a concept including proper prioritizing between 'work' (career and ambition) and 'lifestyle' (health, pleasure, leisure, family and spiritual development/meditation)."

We've all heard this term, "work-life balance" thrown around quite a bit – but is it really something that is achievable? It's the ideal goal of everyone who opens and runs their own small business: Spending enough time at work to be a success in your industry, but also having enough time to be with friends and family, pursue a relaxing hobby, or enjoy an extracurricular activity that you're passionate about.

With this definition in mind, we must now define what makes up the "optimized" balance between your work and lifestyle. Is it exactly a 50/50 split between career and lifestyle choices? Is it so you don't get stressed out managing your small business? Does a work-life balance mean you can go on vacation anytime you want to?

To some degree, this balance is deeply personal and highly individualized to each business owner, but there are some basic principles we should be able to agree on.

For example, good balance means:

- Not working so hard you end up hating your career.
- Taking care of your personal health and wellbeing.
- Making enough time for the activities in life that you truly enjoy.

- Spending enough time with the people who are important to you.
- Achieving what you want to accomplish in your business, without overdoing it.

With these examples in mind, let's look at how to improve your work-life balance.

### *Balancing Act*

To help you find your own work-life balance, we'll explore 12 different things culled from the experience of entrepreneurs and small business owners who have struggled and succeeded.

**1. It's Not About Balance – It's Really About Give-and-Take**
It is not possible to achieve and exact work life balance in a mathematical sense. Trying to do that will probably drive you mad. There will be days when your business will require more time and attention. Conversely, there will be days when your personal life requires more time and attention. Try not to think of splitting your attention between the two evenly, but giving your attention to each as it is needed at a particular point in time.

For instance, when you're first starting out and trying to build your business from the ground up, chances are you'll be spending a lot more time on business-related activities. Your family or personal life may take a back seat as a result.

During this time, try to remember that your business won't always demand this much attention and it always helps to have a good life partner who can step in and take up some of slack on the personal and family front. However, do not forget to step back at regular intervals and recharge - you are of no use to anyone if you are too stressed out to make decisions or you get sick.

**2. Set Boundaries and Keep Them**

The most important boundaries to set for small business owners are those pertaining to work hours. Many entrepreneurs fall into the trap of working around the clock, sacrificing weekends, sleep, family meals and breaks to keep their business going. (Learning how to delegate can be the first line of defense here!)

Attempting to sustain such a pace comes with a high price tag: sleep deprivation and exhaustion. When you're sleep-deprived and exhausted, meeting any kind of expectations becomes a distant memory, and your personal relationships will suffer as well. The following boundaries can help:

**Time:** Set specific work hours and try to adhere to them. Determine which days you're going to take off and stick to them. Embrace personal time and vacation days.

**Space:** Leave your work at the "office," whether it's a room inside your home or a space down the road. For example, I have a client who will complete everything at the office and NOT take her computer home, thus creating a separation between work space and living space. Eat dinner with the family, play with your kids, watch a funny show. Get out of your "work" space and into your 'living' space.

**Access:** There is such a thing as being "too accessible". Determine when you will be accessible for professional and personal inquiries. Of course, be emergencies will crop up, but don't fall into the trap of allowing a client's emergency to become your emergency. Unless a product or service you have provided to the client is failing, chances are you can manage expectations for how long it will take to remedy the situation. The same is true for family and friends. Having constant access to the Internet does not mean you should be available 24/7 to everyone!

**3. When You Say You're Taking Time Off, Take Time Off**
Technology is a blessing and a curse. Because it's easy to quickly check email, call a client or edit a proposal, you may find yourself doing these things on days you've designated as time-off or, even worse, on sick days. If you've told people you're taking time off, honor that commitment to yourself. It will make it easier for others to honor it as well.

**4. Keep Your Social Commitments**
If you've planned to attend a family picnic or a child's school performance, keep those plans. Chances are that nothing will fall apart if you're out of the office for an hour or two, or turn off your phone for the evening. If you feel that you must make the time up, do so after the commitment has been honored.

You should view these types of fun "non-work" events as if they are work events. Give them the same level of importance, put them in your calendar and you'll find it's much easier to consistently make them a priority.

**5. Yes, Even You Deserve a Vacation**
Just as important as setting boundaries is the concept of taking time off, of taking vacation time. This is a great way to reinvigorate yourself and rekindle the motivation to keep working toward your goals. Everyone gets tired and overwhelmed, but rather than overworking yourself even further by trying to power through the fatigue, take a vacation. Consider taking an "unplugged" vacation where you are not checking email and social media every five minutes. Delegate these "check ups" to someone on your team, go on vacation and truly "be present".

**6. Take Care of Yourself**
You'll work better and more effectively if you're healthy and a large of part of your personal health is contingent on eating right and exercising.

If you already have an established routine of gym time or a personal trainer, keep that routine. Don't think that the expectations of your business take priority over everything else.

Yes, there are times where you need to be flexible, but try as hard as you can to keep the time set aside for yourself. You really need to set aside time to plan and execute your food intake – don't give way to the quick fix of using the vending machine down the hall as a good snack choice.

**7. Delegate**

Remember my reference to Michael Gerber, author of the E-Myth in chapter one? He points out that it is important to distinguish between the tasks that only you can perform and tasks that you can ask someone else to handle. If you don't have any employees, then delegating may involve outsourcing relevant tasks to a third party or hiring someone on a part-time basis. If you do have employees, remember that you hired them for a reason.

Ideally, that reason was their competence. Remember that the more you exclusively hold on to projects and tasks, the less likely your employees—and by extension your business—will grow. Employees who feel that there aren't opportunities for growth will eventually leave – and you will be left wearing all the hats.

**8. Remember to Ask for Help**

Chances are you have someone in your life—or a few people if you're lucky—that you go to for help. It could be emotional help, financial help or strategic help, but they provide you with support nonetheless. When you feel yourself starting to get overwhelmed, don't forget to reach out to the folks who are your support system. Even if it's just an excuse to get out of the office for an hour, this respite can make a world of difference to your mood and motivation.

You might also consider finding a business mentor and/or business coach. A good mentor will be willing to guide you through the pitfalls of running a business from their own unique perspective, which can save you time and money, as well as your sanity.

**9. Take Breaks**

It is so important to pace yourself during the workday. It's best to view the hours in the office as a marathon, not a sprint. Step away from your desk for five or 10 minutes. Do some jumping jacks, and go run up and down the stairs.Go outside for a breath of fresh air or a brisk walk. Grab some water from the kitchen and spend a few minutes talking about last night's game with an employee.

No matter what you choose to take as a break from work throughout the day, make it part of your routine and stick to it. One trick: schedule 10- or 15-minute breaks in your calendar at specific times during the day. When you get the reminder that it's time to take a walk around the block, get up and do it. Put as much priority on the break as you do on a client appointment – and the results will surprise you!

**10. Pace Yourself**

Unless you've just invented the ultimate widget that no one can live without, your business will not be built overnight. It will take time to grow your business, build your brand and find ongoing success. As a result, trying to achieve all your business goals in the first six months of hanging up a shingle isn't realistic, and the pace could kill you. Spend time prioritizing your most immediate goals and tasks, with some left over. Don't try to finish everything at once – remember, enjoy the journey.

### 11. Set Your Own Norms

While it's important to understand how other small businesses or entrepreneurs work, embrace the idea that their method for success may not be yours. Don't be a copy cat; focus on the plan, the schedule, the timing and the boundaries that work for you.

### 12. Don't Be Afraid to Say No

This is probably the hardest lesson to learn, but it might be the most important. You will be faced with clients, employees, partners, friends and family who will demand your time and attention for a variety of reasons, some valid, some not.

Before you say no, analyze the request, the time it will take you to fulfill it and the potential return from fulfilling it. If the numbers add up, then maybe figuring out a way to fit the request into your schedule is a good idea. If they don't, you might need to turn them down. If it is a request from family, see if it fits in the parameters that you have set – if it does, say yes – if not say no. Family need to understand what the rules are and live by them every bit as much as you do.

Achieving work-life balance is always challenging - any small business owner will tell you that. However, by setting your boundaries, treating your social commitments as important as your work commitments and seeking help when you need it, you might just be able to find an equilibrium that suits your lifestyle. There is no 'one size fits all'. It is important for you to look at everything in your life and determine what priority each piece deserves – and then stick to it!

### *Attitude, Perspective and Being Present*

One of the favorite slides I have in my keynote presentation is one that says "A bad attitude is like a flat tire – If you don't change it, you will never go anywhere!" Another favorite of mine is "The people who talk about the glass being half empty or half full are missing the point that the glass is refillable."

While the helpful tips I have shared in this chapter will assist you on your journey to clarity, it is really your attitude and perspective that will have the most impact on how your live your life. It may seem very Annie-esk to say 'always look on the bright side of life' but that is truly the way to create a journey worth taking.

Back in my parent's day, a favorite saying was "Take time to stop and smell the roses." This saying is right up there with "enjoy the journey." Both of these sayings are sage advice for the busy entrepreneur.

Another way of saying 'stop and smell the roses' is being fully present in a given moment in time. Technology has us thinking that we are super heroes who can take multi-tasking to all new levels. It is important to develop the ability to truly focus on one thing at a time. Remove distractions if you have to – if you are chatting with your child, then your phone should not be in your hand while you surreptitiously check incoming texts.

Being able to truly experience each moment in time is valuable. You can always make more money, but you cannot make more time, so experience each minute to the fullest. Once it is gone, you will never get it back again.

**Picture Perfect Business Success**

Being present is something that can take much practice for it to become second nature. Our technology driven world has most of us believing that we have to be multi-tasking geniuses to ever get ahead in this world – when in reality, there is no such thing as successful multi-tasking. Yes, you can learn to do several tasks in quick succession, but our brains are really wired to concentrate totally on one thing at a time.

Practice the art of being present no matter what the task or activity. Banish the worry about getting everything done and concentrate on 'being' with your child when they ask a question. Then get back to your task at hand – concentrating fully on it. Social media cannot become a distractor is we close them while concentrating on a particular job.

Being present it not hard – it is just simply something that we forget to practice. We let the ever growing 'to do' list overwhelm us, and the worry about not getting everything done actually becomes a fulfilled prophecy because the worry takes over and we forget to concentrate on the task in front of us! Keep it simple – be present, and just focus on one thing at a time.

"Drink your tea slowly and reverently, as if it is the axis
on which the world earth revolves – slowly, evenly, without
rushing toward the future. Live the actual moment.
Only this moment is life."

~Thich Nhat Hanh

# Section Three

## Mission – Putting the Puzzle Together

# Chapter Five

## Create Clarity of Business goals

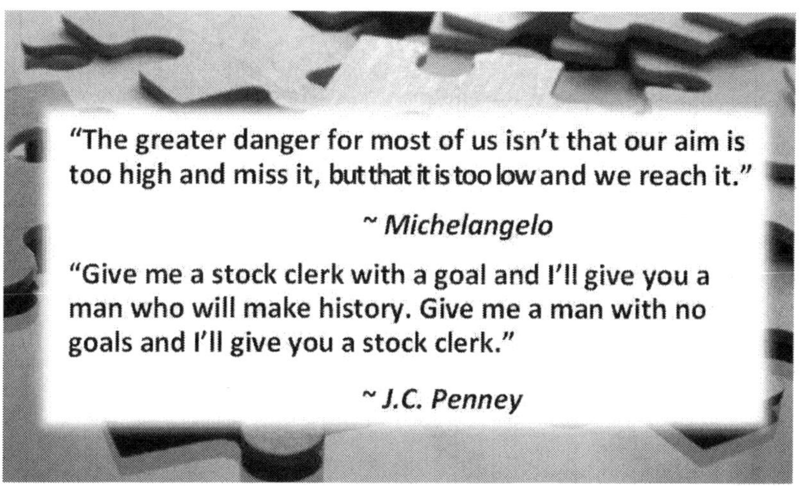

"The greater danger for most of us isn't that our aim is too high and miss it, but that it is too low and we reach it."
~ Michelangelo
"Give me a stock clerk with a goal and I'll give you a man who will make history. Give me a man with no goals and I'll give you a stock clerk."
~ J.C. Penney

If you give someone a bow and arrow and tell them to, "SHOOT!" their first response would probably be, "Shoot at what?" When there is no target, there is no purpose for shooting. So, if the person shoots the arrow, then wherever the arrow lands is where it lands and nothing specific will have been accomplished.

However, if you give the archer a target and challenged him to hit the bullseye – everything changes. You now gave him something to aim at, something to challenge his skills against, something to measure his progress with, and something that gives all of his effort – purpose. All by adding in a simple target.

That's what a goal does to your life – It changes everything. It gives you something to aim for and something to measure against. It gives you that all important GPS guidance that is always checking where you are at any given point in time and referencing that against the ultimate destination.

Everybody in this world has a different set of circumstances, different set of skills, and a different set of opportunities through which they can interact with the world and find their unique sense of fulfillment. Your mission in life should be to figure out what your unique, "sets" are and how you can best capitalize on them to give your effort purpose and meaning. Goals are the guiding light that get you to where you have you want to go.

Just keep in mind that while creating the picture on the box (establishing your vision) is the important first step, you still need to put the puzzle pieces together (creating clarity of business goals).

***Looking Back***

Take some time right now to reflect on some of your goals in the past. Think about some of your New Year's Resolutions that you never saw through to the end and some of the resolutions that you actually did succeed in keeping, either personally or for your business.

Remember how it felt to realize you had met your goal? That rush of positive energy when you realized you had kept on track and had reached your destination - you were then ready to tackle even harder goals!

However, the opposite can happen if you keep setting goals and then not keeping them. The negative energy generated by the disappointment you feel when you fail to meet a goal can really derail your personal energy and ultimately derail your business.

### *First Step*

Alright, you have the picture on the box of what you want your business to become in the future. You have crafted your vision statement and created your vision board. Now, you need a game plan for how to put the pieces together to create the finished product. One of the first steps is to look at what specifics make up a good company.

From a general perspective, a good company will:

### *Have a Code of Ethics and a Positive Attitude*

Have you ever heard the saying that your attitude determines your altitude? Gone are the days when owners of companies followed the 'walk softly and carry a big stick' code of business building. Having a positive attitude and knowing how to engender that attitude in others is a very important aspect to growing a successful business.

And, it is important to back up that positive attitude with a basic code of ethics. The basics of keeping your word and following the golden rule will never go out of style. While it may be tempting to make an unethical short-term decision for instant profit, the long term affects always out way any short-term gain.

### *Have a specific focus and a workable plan*

Really know and understand what business you are in and what you provide to your customers. Having clarity of thought is important to ensure that you, your employees and your customers know what to expect. Make sure you are concentrating on what you do well, even when you expand.

***The Owners and Managers need to have Passion, Ambition and Risk Assessment/Management***

To truly be successful, a company must have people at the helm who are motivated by something other than just money and financial success. They must have a passion for what they are doing, and be fueled by the love they have for the business to the point that it will carry them through the tough times.

Business owners who are passionate enough about their business to take risks stand to gain the most and grow the most. However, it is important to understand that you need to put the word 'calculated' in front of the word risk.

Risk without calculation is merely gambling! Business owners need to be flexible and ready to jump aboard when technology and/or culture changes, yet avoid taking risks without the necessary planning.

***Culture of Commitment to Employees and Customers***

Company culture is one of the most important characteristics of a successful business. A successful business will have workers who are suited for the positions that they hold, with policies to motivate them to continue working well at those positions and staying focused on playing nicely with others. The necessary positive attitude of the owners needs to seep down to all layers of the business.

***Education and Assessment must be a priority***

Beyond making a business a great place to work, business owners need to be committed to spending the time and resources necessary to get the training that their employees need to 'keep up with the times.' Continually looking for opportunities to update training and education opportunities needs to be an integral part of the business plan.

### *Implementing the Vision*

Your mission statement is all about how you are going to put the puzzle together so that your business aligns with your vision. Mission statements define the organization's purpose and primary objectives. These statements are set in the present tense, and they explain why you exist as a business, both to members of the organization and to people outside it.

Mission statements tend to be short, clear and powerful. A vision statements defines the organization's purpose and focuses on its goals and aspirations. These statements are designed to be uplifting and inspiring. Usually they are timeless. Vision is the picture on the box and the mission includes why you drew the picture in the first place.

## How to Write Your Mission Statement

Your mission statement explains what your business must do on a day-to-day basis to make your vision statement a reality. It is putting the puzzle together according to the picture on the box. It is practical and rooted in the present. Basically, the mission statement will give you guidance any time you wonder, "What should I do today?" or "How should I act today?"

Because it has a practical focus, a mission statement is easier to write than a vision statement. (You have already done the hard part of defining that your business should look like in the future.) With your vision statement to hand, ask yourself, "What must I do to make this happen?"

As a rule, mission statements tend to be customer-focused, so another way of asking the question is: "What must I do for my customers to make my vision for my business a reality?"

Susan Ward, a business writer and a regular contributor to the online site 'the balance', defines the mission statement as something that "articulates a company's purpose – it announces to the world at large why your company exists." She goes on to say that she feels a mission statement is a combination of what your business does and WHY it does it, expressed in a way that encapsulates the values that are important to you and the company.

Tim Barry, founder of Palo Alto Software and a regular contributor to Bplans, has many words of wisdom to share on the subject of crafting a usable mission statement. The steps below are a summary of his ideas.

***Step One – Have a Story that Defines your Market***

You don't really have to write a story but think about a real person making the decision to buy what you have to offer – use your imagination to see why they want to buy from you, and what does that do for them.

The more specific the story, the better. The good stories really explain the need or want, the essential "why they buy" and the all-important reason why your business is different. You need to be able to articulate why your business is unique and be clear on what it does and what it does NOT do.

***Step Two - Define what your business specifically does for its customers***

Start your mission statement with the good you do. Use your market-defining story to explain the specifics of what it is that makes your business special for your target customer.

Don't undervalue your business- identify all the things that set you apart, that make you special and what benefits you specifically provide to your clients. Be very clear and don't grandstand. If you feel your company 'is good for planet' be very specific about why you think so.

For example, Apple Computer's 2017 mission statement is:

"Apple designs Macs, the best personal computers in the world, along with OS X, iLife, iWork and professional software. Apple leads the digital music revolution with its iPods and iTunes online store. Apple has reinvented the mobile phone with its revolutionary iPhone and App store and is defining the future of mobile media and computing devices with iPad."

Nobody could mistake that this mission statement with generic advertising hype. And it's an interesting change from the early mission as defined by founder Steve Jobs:

"To make a contribution to the world by making tools for the mind that advance humankind."

So, you can see how Apple's Mission got more specific over time, making it a more meaningful.

***Step Three - Define what your business does for its employees***
Good businesses must be good for their employees too or they will not survive. Retaining employees is better for the bottom line than high turnover. Company culture matters and rewarding and motivating people matters. A mission statement can define what your business offers its employees, and outlines what important qualities are emphasized such as fairness, diversity, respect for creativity and ideas, training, providing the right tools, and overall empowerment. (And, don't just say these things, include action steps!)

If you have a special view on your relationship with employees, write it into the mission statement. If your business is friendly to families, or to remote virtual workplaces, put that into your mission. Making employees a priority is rare in mission statements. Most mission statements are focused on messaging for customers.

American Express, however, includes the team in its mission:

"We have a mission to be the world's most respected service brand. To do this, we have established a culture that supports our team members, so they can provide exceptional service to our customers."

***Step Four - Be specific on what the business does for its owners***
Some would say that it goes without saying that a business exists to enhance the financial position of its owners, and maybe it does. However, the mission statement needs to include the overall intent not just the need to make money.

Some of the best mission statements incorporate a much broader sense of mission that includes, or at least implies, the mission of ownership and what intent they have to make a difference.

Warby Parker, an eyewear company, does a great job at voicing a higher mission that includes customers, employees, and owners.

"Warby Parker was founded with a rebellious spirit and a lofty objective: to offer designer eyewear at a revolutionary price, while leading the way for socially-conscious business."

Mission Statements are Organic – Continually feed, prune and revise!

Good mission statements serve multiple functions, define objectives, and live for a long time. So, don't be afraid to edit, prune and update as changes warrant it.

As you edit, keep a sharp eye out for the buzzwords and hype that everybody else used – you need to select words with care to ensure your unique attributes are showcased. Cut as much as you can that doesn't apply to your business. Unique itself, the word, means literally, the only one in the world. Use it sparingly.

Phrases such as "being the best possible," "world-class," and "great customer service" mean little because everybody uses them – and they are hard to quantify. Having great customer service is way harder than writing that into a mission statement.

Susan Ward gives great examples of how mission statements can be distilled and edited for more clarity.

"When you're finished, have another look at your mission statement and see if it says what you want to say or if there's a better way of phrasing it. Be sure to change the phrase "my company's purpose" to the name of your company.

"My company's purpose is to grow market vegetables using organic, sustainable farming practices to give people safe and healthy food choices",

might be rephrased to produce this finished mission statement:

"At Earth's Bounty, we grow market vegetables in a way that's good for the earth and good for the table."

And, for the rest of your business's life, review and revise your mission statement as needed. As with everything else in a business plan, your mission statement should never be written in stone. It needs to be reviewed and updated on a regular basis to stay relevant and it needs to be visible to be useful.

***How to Keep on Course***

When you look at business texts, they talk about 'leak'. This is the concept of getting off course and doing things that are not aligned with your core mission. However, I prefer to use the word 'drift'.

A good friend of mine is on the board of a halfway house where the mission is to provide services to high school boys. Drift or leak would occur if they decided to establish and open a halfway home for drug addicts of all ages or to provide mental health or other geriatric services for the elderly. These services would drift from the original purpose and mission and if not held in check, the organization can spend a considerable amount of time pursuing goals and tasks that, albeit may be altruistic and meaningful, fail to be aligned with the organization's original mission and purpose.

***Putting the Mission Statement into Action***

You have created the picture on the puzzle box (vision) for your business and you have created your mission statement (high level statement of how you are going to reach your visions.) Now it's time to create the step-by-step approach on how you are going to live and work each day to ensure that you reach your ultimate destination.

***Tried but True Approach***

If you have spent any time looking or studying business, then you will have seen the SMART approach to establishing goals. Of course, there is the obvious play on words that your goals need to be smart (as in intelligent) while at the same time, be Specific, Measurable, Achievable, Realistic and Timely.

In very simple terms, goals provide the motivational energy to carry on even when motivation is low.

The SMART way of expressing how to establish goals has become the 'norm' in the business world. The acronym encourages us to make goals specific, measurable, agreed-upon (some people use achievable or attainable), realistic and time-bound.

While the concept of business goals was discussed as far back as the late 19th century, it was the well-known American Philosopher Elbert Hubbard who began to study why people failed at their endeavors in business. He discovered that they failed, not because they were lacking in intelligence or were not brave enough to try, but that they did not have an organized way to set or achieve their goals.

It is generally accepted that the SMART acronym was first written down in November 1981 in Spokane, Washington. George T. Doran, a consultant and former Director of Corporate Planning for Washington Water Power Company published a paper titled

"There's a S.M.A.R.T. Way to Write Management's Goals and Objectives".

In his paper, Doran provides some clarification for readers on applying the SMART acronym:

"Managers are confused by all the verbal from seminars, books, magazines, consultants, and so on. Let me suggest therefore, that when it comes to writing effective objectives (goals), corporate officers, managers, and supervisors just have to think of the acronym SMART. Ideally speaking, each corporate, department and section objective should be: (SMART).

***George T. Doran***

Many people believe that effective goals and objectives must incorporate all five elements of SMART. However, Doran explains, that the suggested acronym doesn't mean that every objective written will have all five criteria.

For example, not everything worth achieving is measurable. And a goal you set for yourself does not need to be agreed-upon.

The SMART Definition

SMART does not have one definitive meaning. In fact, the words within the acronym have changed over time. And they continue to vary somewhat depending on the person using the term.

Doran's original definition tied in five criteria:

Specific: target a specific area for improvement.

Measurable: quantify, or at least suggest, an indicator of progress.

Assignable: specify who will do it.

Realistic: state what results can realistically be achieved given available resources.

Time-related: specify when the result can be achieved.

He saw that by helping people focus their attention in these five areas, they would improve their chances of success. Over the years, people have substituted some of the original words with different terms that meet their specific needs – and the concept still works for them.

SMART goals have provided a clear and simple recipe for defining and managing goals and objectives. The acronym works well; people find it easy to remember and it is useful – hence its popularity almost a half of a century after the concept was created.

This concept clearly outlines that goals need to be specific and measurable to have any value. If you have no way of measuring your success, how do you know you have arrived your goal? Basic logic continually reinforces why SMART goals are necessary. SMART goals can be used by anyone, anywhere, without the need for any tools or training. However, while writing a SMART goal can be easy, sticking to it can be the hard part.

Write your SMART goals down on paper. Keep them in your pocket. Refer to them frequently to check you are making progress toward achieving your goals. Make sure it is something that will get you out of bed in the morning, something that drives your passion.

***The Critics***

Not everyone sees SMART goals as a ultimate force in goal setting. Some critics argue that the SMART technique doesn't work well for long-term goals because it lacks flexibility. However, it is up to the person setting the goals to establish how flexibility will be introduced. And, of course, just setting a goal does not guarantee success. It takes passion, creativity and commitment to ensure SMART goals are successful.

Whether in business or your personal life, it is the well thought out goals and objectives that help you achieve the best possible result. Using the SMART framework can help you make sure your goals becomes reality and they do not end up in a graveyard of missed opportunities.

***Goal Setting Summary***

The bottom line is this – if you want your business to succeed, you need to establish goals. Sometimes people shy away from writing goals down because then they are afraid they will fail. While the concept of accountability is important, it is also important to establish a 'friendly room' – people who will help you accomplish your goals and not judge you when you fail at attaining a specific one.

Use the SMART framework to sketch out your goals, then tailor them to fit your unique situation. Be brave and make up some of the rules as you go along!

"Our goals can only be reached through a vehicle of a plan, in which we must fervently believe, and upon which we must vigorously act. There is no other route to success." ~ Pablo Picasso

"A goal properly set is halfway reached." ~ Zig Ziglar

# Chapter Six

## Using Clarity of Communication to Accomplish Your Business Goals

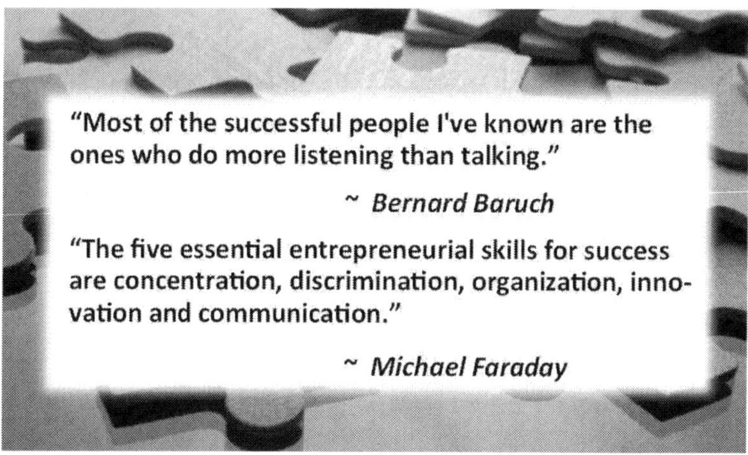

"Most of the successful people I've known are the ones who do more listening than talking."
~ Bernard Baruch
"The five essential entrepreneurial skills for success are concentration, discrimination, organization, innovation and communication."
~ Michael Faraday

"Communication is Everything!" Lee Iacocca made this statement in his book Iacocca, and many others have made similar claims to highlight the necessary skills needed to excel and inspire as a leader and business owner.

Effective communication transcends every aspect of our business and personal lives. What you can accomplish as a business person, parent, friend, educator, customer, client or supplier is highly dependent on your ability to get the message across. Probably 99% of the problems within organizations are caused by a breakdown or failure in the communication process.

Many people believe that those who can text at lightning speed, plow through emails, blog consistently or speak loud, fast and have no problem talking with others on any subject, are effective communicators. In fact, the opposite is often true. Being able to quickly string words together does not mean the message is understood by others.

### *Communication Basics*

To effectively get your message across, start with these Three Communication Basics:

Be Clear: Clarity saves time, money and mistakes. Answer the question that is being asked. Ask for the information you desire. Too often people beat around the bush or go off on a tangent and the real issues are not addressed. Additionally, if you are providing instructions, provide details and expectations. Assuming the recipient knows what you want can lead to disappointment on both sides.

Know Your Audience: Perspective is based on an individual and that individual may not look at things the same way you do. Consider who you are communicating with. Think about where the other person is coming from. What is his point of view? What are her problems or concerns? What is he trying to accomplish? What is her level of knowledge or information?

Listen: Perhaps the most overstated and under practiced element of all is listening. Listening shows respect and indicates that what the individual must convey is important.

It also allows you to get information. Let people complete a thought before responding. Most of us are already forming a response before we even hear the full thought or read the full message. Key information is often missed.

The first thing we are taught about effective communication is to listen. "Listen with feeling;" "Hear what is being said." But what if we could also see what is being said? Centuries of communication research and observation reveal that impactful, influential communication consists of:

- 7% WORDS
- 38% TONE of VOICE
- 55% GESTURES/BODY LANGUAGE

We spend hours planning what to say, painstakingly choosing words to position ourselves and our products, services or ideas in the most effective way. We spend additional hours analyzing the words of others, attempting to determine the "real meaning." While words and tone of voice are important, these convey less than half the message.

***Who Are You Communicating With?***

When it comes to communicating for maximum success in your business, there are two main concepts that must be made a priority – WHO are you communicating with and HOW are you communicating?

Let's have a look at the WHO first.

You are going to be communicating with your employees, your customers, various audiences of potential customers and competitors. Each of these main categories can then be broken down into subsets by age.

Much is made these days of millennial's and their addictions to smart phones and social media. But they're not the only ones who have preferences about how they like to communicate.

Just ask Haydn Shaw, expert in generational differences. In his book Sticking Points, Shaw breaks down the differences and similarities between the most predominant generations today. There are four categories to consider: Millennial's reach 22 to 37, (on a quick side note, Millennial's became the largest group in Q1 of 2015, surpassing Gen Xers as the largest generation in US labor force.) Gen Xers aged 38 to 53, Boomers age 54 to 72, and Traditionalists age 73 and older.

The key to successful in cross generational communication, Shaw says, is to figure out the language of the other generations and try to speak it. WHEN you were born definitely makes a difference in HOW you communicate. Let's have a look at a quick overview of each category.

**Traditionalists**

What they're like:

This generation grew up learning cursive writing in the age of print media and radio.

Messaging was one-way, with traditionalists often looking to experts to get the facts.

What they've experienced:

Traditionalists lived through to world wars, the great depression and prohibition.

They experienced the first popular talking movie, the jazz singer, and read headlines about the United States dropping an atomic bomb on Hiroshima in August 1945.

How best to communicate with Traditionalists:

Have an in person, face-to-face conversation.

Shut off your phone, lean back and offer them your undivided attention.

But don't completely neglect digital communication.

Shaw explains that older generations are rapidly adopting smart phones and social media to stay connected.

**Baby Boomers**

What they're like:

Boomers grew up with television, and rather than experts relating facts for consumption, entertainers persuaded the baby boomer audience with messages that were more the visual.

What they've experienced:

In addition to television, Baby Boomers experienced the civil rights movement, the Vietnam conflict and Watergate. The release of the Feminine Mystique sparked second wave feminism, and hundreds of thousands attended Woodstock in 1969.

How best to communicate with Baby Boomers:

Pick up the phone and call baby boomers. It's how they made plans and asked one another out on dates.

**Gen Xers**

What they're like:

Growing up with digital communication, Gen Xers had access to multiple sources of information and therefore could do their own research to double check the facts they were given.

What they've experienced:

Gen Xers were the first to experience double-digit inflation.

Major headlines included the Iran hostage crisis, the Challenger explosion and the tearing down of the Berlin wall. In the entertainment world, the first Sony Walkman was released, and the launch of MTV changed how music was consumed.

How best to communicate with Gen Xers:

Send an email. Gen Xers are attuned to the sound of logging onto instant messaging and other web-based applications.

**Millennial's**

What they're like:

Unlike Traditionalists and Baby Boomers, this generation grew up with two-way, interactive communication, so they expect to participate and to be heard.

What they've experienced:

Millennial's grew up seeing Columbine, the September 11 attacks, the great recession and the occupy Wall Street movement. Barack Obama became the first African-American president elected in 2008, and same-sex marriage became legal in all 50 states in 2015.

How best to communicate with Millennials:

Quick and easy. Millennial's like to be communicated with via text message, instant message and social networking sites. Shaw explains that when connecting with Millennial's, if you stay in contact with them through text that they will stay in contact with you in other ways as well.

## Generation Z

The next generation to enter the workforce in great numbers will be Gen Z. According to the U.S. Census Bureau, Gen Z will make up 25 percent of the population. However, there are many pivotal differences between Millennials and Generation Z that will affect organizational structure, workplace communication, employee training and much more!

These pivotal differences include a realistic outlook on how hard they will have to work to get ahead, a very independent spirit, total upbringing in a digital world, more selective in what they share online, and a shift back to more face-to-face communication vs. digital only. (Although Instagram is still their social media platform of choice). They understand the need for soft skills and the ability to move within an organization instead of simply job-hopping. They have a more entrepreneur spirit and they consider themselves Global citizens instead of merely Global spectators.

### *How Are You Communicating?*

If you are trying to communicate with everyone in the same way, you are missing the boat! It is extremely important to learn how to be a 'chameleon' and adapt to any situation when dealing with employees, customers, connectors and competitors.

There are many types of personalities and communication styles. I use DiSC® in my coaching practice, an assessment tool that helps you build more effective working relationships based on an understanding of different behavioral styles. I ask all my clients to take a 30-minute online DiSC® assessment that gives me a wealth of information about their behavior style.

DiSC® stands for: Dominance (sees the big picture, direct), Influence (enthusiastic, collaborative), Steadiness (calm, supportive), Conscientiousness (independent, objective). We are all a blend of the DiSC® styles, but usually one or two styles stand out.

DiSC® is the leading personal assessment tool used by over 1 million people every year to improve work productivity, teamwork and communication.

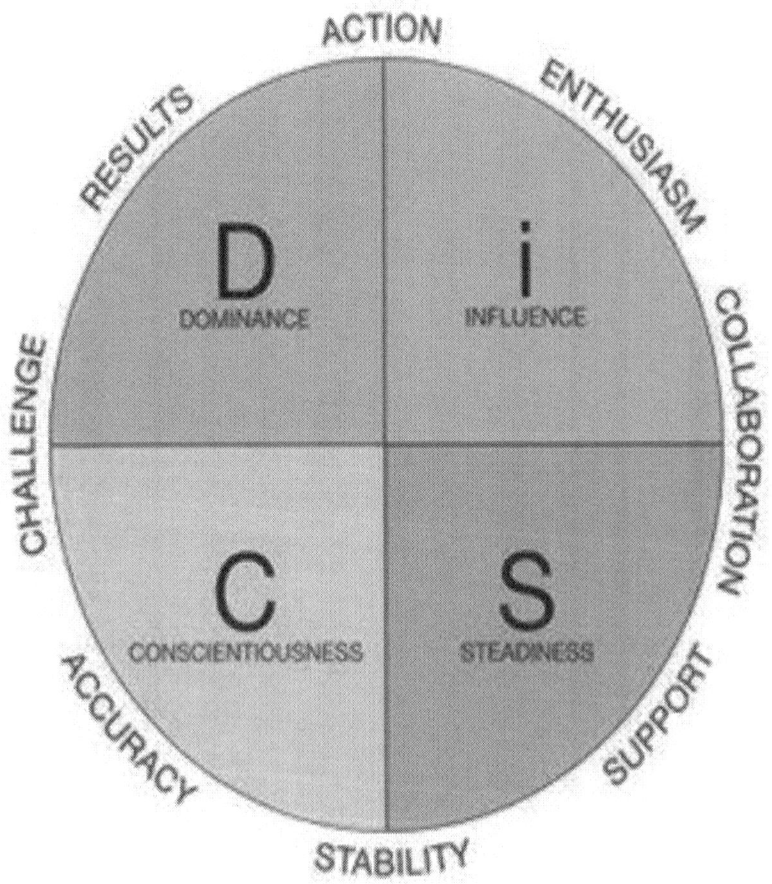

The DiSC® profile, published by Wiley, is a non-judgmental tool used for discussion of people's behavioral differences. I ask very one of my clients to complete a series of questions that produces a detailed report about their personality and behavior.

This report also gives tips related to working with people of other styles.

The DiSC® model provides a common language that people can use to better understand themselves and adapt their behaviors with others - within a work team, a sales relationship, a leadership position, or other relationships.

DiSC® profiles help you and your team:

- Increase your self-knowledge: how you respond to conflict, what motivates you, what causes you stress and how you solve problems
- Improve working relationships by recognizing the communication needs of team members
- Facilitate better teamwork and teach productive conflict
- Develop stronger sales skills by identifying and responding to customer styles
- Manage more effectively by understanding the dispositions and priorities of employees and team members
- Become more self-knowledgeable, well-rounded and effective leaders.

What does DiSC® stand for? What do the letters mean?

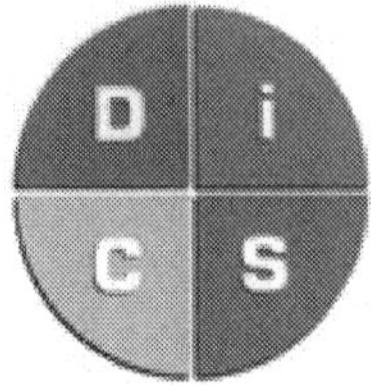


**Dominance**

Person places emphasis on accomplishing results, the bottom line, confidence

Behaviors
- Sees the big picture
- Can be blunt
- Accepts challenges
- Gets straight to the point

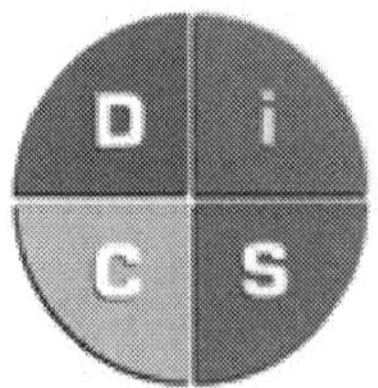


**Influence**

Person places emphasis on influencing or persuading others, openness, relationships

Behaviors
- Shows enthusiasm
- Is optimistic
- Likes to collaborate
- Dislikes being ignored

**Steadiness**

Person places emphasis on cooperation, sincerity, dependability

Behaviors
- Doesn't like to be rushed
- Calm manner
- Calm approach
- Supportive actions

**Conscientiousness**

Person places emphasis on quality and accuracy, expertise, competency

Behaviors
- Enjoys independence
- Objective reasoning
- Wants the details
- Fears being wrong

### *Know Your Audience*

How many times have you lost an important negotiation and wondered why? It could be because you are communicating the same way to everyone. But, you could be missing as much as 75% of your opportunities by doing this. Everyone receives information differently. Behavior, personality, environment, skills, role, and emotions all affect how people give and receive information.

However, it is possible to increase your communication success with the people you are currently missing the mark with by taking into consideration who you are talking to. These guidelines will improve your ability to get the message across to anyone by simply observing behavior first.

***When you observe someone who is:***

Decisive, tough, impatient, strong-willed, competitive, demanding, independent, direct, does not listen

DO: give immediate feedback, concentrate on the subject, focus on the results

DON'T: frustrate desire to take action, restrict power, spend time on non-essentials

COMMUNICATION TIPS: pick up the pace; be direct, brief and to the point; stick to business; use a logical approach; focus on results, not tactics; identify opportunities and challenges; do not touch or get too close; do not be emotional; act quickly; let him/her win

Sociable, talkative, open, enthusiastic, energetic, persuasive, spontaneous, emotional, talks more than listens

DO: show enthusiasm, smile, chat, focus on the positive, make it fun, let him/her talk

DON'T: discourage enthusiasm, focus on the details, react negatively

COMMUNICATION TIPS: allow time for socializing, have fun, ask for feelings and opinions, create a friendly environment, be friendly and warm, give recognition; talk about people and feelings, use touch (forearm, back).

Calm, steady, laid back, careful, patient, amiable, listens carefully, is sincere, modest, indecisive and trustworthy

DO: slow down, take your time, provide assurance and support, give enough time to decide

DON'T: be restless or impatient, press for action, make sudden changes, fail to deliver on promises.

COMMUNICATION TIPS: be patient, build trust, draw out opinions, present issues logically, relax and allow time for discussion, show how solutions benefit him/her, define all areas, provide plenty of information, secure commitment step-by-step, involve him/her in the planning.

Precise, exact, analytical, logical, systematic, quiet, careful, formal, disciplined, does not express emotions.

DO: give details, answer all questions patiently, give time to think and decide.

DON'T: keep information to yourself, pressure for decisions, be too chatty.

COMMUNICATION TIPS: use data/facts, stay on task, focus on quality, use proven ideas, do not touch, be patient, slow down, avoid personal issues, explain clearly and carefully.

Once you identify your audience, apply these simple communication approaches and watch your success begin to soar!

***Who am I? D***

You are about to interview/network with a person who is ambitious, forceful, strong-willed, independent and goal oriented.

This person is a director D.

They are fast talkers. They are quick decision-makers.

They are big risk takers.

They have a strong sense of urgency.

Their hot button is: time, results, productivity, profits.

Behavior style examples

Arnold Schwarzenegger and Barbara Walters.

The D Behavior Style tends to be direct and decisive, sometimes described as dominant. They would prefer to lead than follow and tend towards leadership and management positions. They tend to have high self-confidence and are risk takers and problem solvers, which enables others to look to them for decisions and direction. They tend to be self-starters.

***Who am I? I***

You are about to interview/network with a person who is magnetic, enthusiastic, friendly and demonstrative.

This person is an influencer letter I.

They are very optimistic by nature.

They are smooth and frequent talkers.

They are extroverted in terms of body language.

They want to be liked and respected.

Their hot button is: testimonials, who else bought from them.

Behavior style examples

Oprah Winfrey and Bill Clinton

They love recognition and being the center of attention.

When I'm having coffee with a person who is an I and it's 60 minutes long, I will only talk for 15 minutes.

Station WIIFM, what's in it for me. At the end of the conversation they get the feeling they like me because I made it all about them.

***Who am I? S***

You are about to interview/network with a person who is patient, predictable, reliable, steady, relaxed and modest.

This person is a relator/steady S.

They are slow talkers.

They are slow decision-makers.

They are low risk takers.

Their number one value and hot button is security.

For themselves, their family and their job.

Behavior style examples

Robert Herjavec and Laura Bush.

Laura Bush for obvious reasons. She was a librarian, a political wife and a mother, all things that required patience, reliability and a steady demeanor.

Robert Herjavec from the Shark Tank is an entrepreneur.

He sits on the far-right end of the panel.

He usually waits for the other sharks to make an offer because his behavior style is steady.

He usually has his arms folded in a closed position.

It takes a longer time for him to make a decision because the behavior style characteristics are to gather as much information as possible before making a decision.

It takes a longer time for them to know like and trust you.

***Who am I? C***

You are about to interview/network with a person who is dependent, neat, conservative, perfectionist and cautious.

This person is an analyzer/compliance C.

They are very introverted by nature.

They need as many facts as possible.

The greatest fears being wrong.

Their motto "In God we trust, and all others use data".

Their hot button is: facts, information, precision, details, numbers.

Behavior style examples

Bill Gates and Albert Einstein

They want to know the why behind what they do.

The standard tendencies for C-style people is that they are questioning and skeptical, as well as cautious and reflective. They value high standards, careful analysis and diplomacy. They might shy away from new ideas or respond poorly to criticism of their work. In the workplace they tend to seek the analytical tasks they can complete on their own. You seldom see them making small talk.

### *Making DISC® Work for You*

Anyone can memorize a list of definitions. However, when it comes to making DiSC® work in the everyday world, the true power comes in truly understanding each of the behavior styles and becoming good at identifying specific aspects in people you communicate with (not everyone will be up for taking the DiSC® assessment.)

I have heard people criticize such things as DiSC®, calling them "manipulative". Robert Rohm, a top author and speaker, makes the distinction between manipulation and "influence". He points out that everyone is trying to influence someone to do something – from a mom making a delicious dinner to influence her family to eat better to stores putting out their most attractive clothing to get you to buy.

However, the pivotal point to remember is motivation. When you are influencing someone in a positive manner by your actions and you are trying to help them have a better life, a better attitude or a better relationship, then utilizing your knowledge regarding an assessment like DiSC® can be a positive thing. If you are using it to deceive someone, then obviously it's a negative action.

Communication is important – but so is motivation. Next time you are dealing with a person in business, take a step back and analyze your motive. Check to see if you are truly trying to make their life better and are you being a positive influencer, or are you simply using your influence for personal gain. You can use tools such as DISC® to control the narrative and ensure communication takes place. It also gives you the information you need to evaluate the person you are interacting with to determine future actions.

## Implementing Your Goals with Clear Communication

At the basic root of most humans is the fundamental need to be accepted and be considered 'good' at what they do. When it comes to employees, when goals and targets are communicated clearly, and they feel that they can have some input to the outcome, then 9 times out of 10 the goals will be understood and achieved.

When it comes to communicating with your various audiences as a business, your goal should always be to understand who you are communicating with and what is their behavior style. The more you understand about them, the more effective you will be in communicating your message.

Once everyone is on the same page in the same book, magic happens! You will find your goals falling into place and your business will begin to resemble the picture on the box.

### *Clarity of Communication is Key*

Communication is a key ingredient of creating a successful business. Understanding different behavior perspectives can give you the clarity you need in understanding how to communicate with your different audiences.

I am reminded of a story about the five blind men and the elephant. The first blind man reaches out and puts his hands on the elephant's trunk and says, "An elephant is like a snake." The next blind man reaches out and places his hands on the elephant's ears and says, "No, an elephant is like a dinner plate." The next blind man reaches out and grab a leg and says "No, an elephant is like a tree trunk." The next man reaches out and touches the elephant's side and says "No, it's like the side of a barn." The fifth blind man reaches out and grabs on to the elephant's tail and says "No, an elephant is like a rope."

At the end of the day, all five blind men will have to get together and share their information in order for them to form a true picture of what an elephant looks like!

Getting to clarity in communication with your customers, your employees and your suppliers is a very important part of creating clarity in your business. When you analyze it, much of the confusion in business comes from bad communication.

### *Habits of Highly Successful Communicators*

I've worked with a lot of professionals over the years, and I've noticed quite a few habits that seem to be universal among the most successful of them. These habits are the foundation of every highly effective communicator.

**1. Uses a coach and Continually Grows**
The best communicators believe in what they do. So much so, in fact, they employ the services of a coach themselves in an effort to stay on track and continuously improve.

**2. Lives in the moment and Listens**
You won't see a great communicator staring at their phone when other people are around. They remain focused on the present moment, taking in everything and everyone around them. They are actually listening, not just looking for an opportunity to reply.

**3. Comprehends and Asks questions**
A great communicator is as curious as a cat, asking questions of everyone for no other reason than a sincere interest in getting to know people better on a deeper level.

**4. Genuinely cares**
Empathy is a common characteristic of great communicators. They understand and feel what others are thinking and feeling in a deep and profound way.

**5. Develops trust**

You know the person who you'd trust with your deepest, darkest secrets? The one who'd listen without judgement and who'd never betray you? That person would probably be a great communicator. Also, people do business with people they know, like and trust.

**6. Communicates with Clarity**

Being able to communicate clearly and respectfully with people of varying personalities is a habit they must develop. Likewise, they expect the same in return.

**7. Is confident**

When someone has confidence in their skills and abilities, others are more inclined to follow them. Great communicators know this, and that's why they make it a habit to be self-assured.

**8. Lacks ego**

Successful communicators are confident, but never arrogant. They're uninterested in giving advice or providing solutions, but get very excited by helping others arrive at their own conclusions and solve their own problems.

**9. Is Unafraid and Inspires action**

Can you motivate and others simply by having a conversation with them? Do people feel empowered to tackle their problems after spending time with you? Can you always ask the tough questions? Then you've developed one of the most important habits of a successful communicator.

**10. Remains positive**

Negative self-talk, constant complaining, belittling, and berating? No way. Effective communicators are people who always look on the bright side and offer up encouraging words.  They exude positive energy!

# Chapter Seven

## Creating Raving Fans, an AVATAR and a Buzz

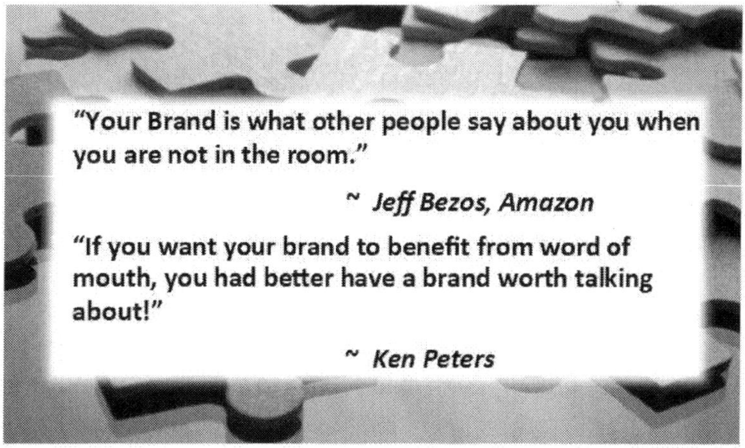

"Your Brand is what other people say about you when you are not in the room."
~ Jeff Bezos, Amazon
"If you want your brand to benefit from word of mouth, you had better have a brand worth talking about!"
~ Ken Peters

Ken Blanchard wrote an amazing book called "Raving Fans: A Revolutionary Approach to Customer Service". This book gives a great synopsis of why raving fans are so important. "Your customers are only satisfied because their expectations are so low and because no one else is doing better. Just having satisfied customers isn't good enough anymore. If you really want a booming business, you have to create Raving Fans."

The final step in creating clarity for your business is to have a clear plan on how you are going to create raving fans. You have established what you are passionate about, created a purpose statement, (identified your WHY) established your vision (created the picture on the box) written your mission (strategy and goals) – now it's time to bring all of those things together to create raving fans, create an AVATAR and most of all, create a BUZZ about your business.

***The Basic Rules of Branding***

Creating a buzz about your business needs to begin with establishing a strong brand. When you hear the word 'brand' it is tempting to just think that a brand is an image, such as the 'Golden Arches' of McDonalds. However, a true brand is much more than just a catchy logo.

The Business Dictionary defines a brand as a "Unique design, sign, symbol, words, or a combination of these, employed in creating an image that identifies a product and differentiates it from its competitors. Over time, this image becomes associated with a level of credibility, quality, and satisfaction in the consumer's mind."

Branding is the process that a company goes through to give meaning to specific products and/or services that are called to mind by consumers via emblems and specific messaging. It is the strategy employed to help people identify specific products, services or even an organization that gives the consumer the reason why they would choose that brand over the competitor's. Your branding messaging needs to be clear, concise and unique – there can be no confusion about what it is or is not.

In branding, the objective is to attract and retain loyal customers by delivering a product or service that is always aligned with what the brand promises in its messaging. Remember, perception is reality. Your message needs to be crystal clear and memorable – and you must ensure that your business can deliver on the promise contained in your branding.

Branding is one of the areas a business focuses on in order to differentiate itself from the competition and stay profitable. Without a strong brand, the businesses we remember growing up with would not be successful. To build a successful business, you need to get your branding right and your branding efforts should include the following:

- **Appealing Design**

While various aspects of design can be subjective, there are design rules that need to be followed in order to communicate the essence of your brand. If you are a company that organizes things, but your logo has a 'messy' design, then your brand will be at odds with your service. Overall design, color choice – every aspect of the printed version of your brand needs to communicate your core values.

- **Consistency**

Being consistent with the application of your logo/brand/identity is very important. How your clients experience your visual brand will affect how they view your business. Establishing and keeping a good perception is all important. All of your content whether in the real world or online should be consistent.

The experience your clients get from your brand will shape their perception of your business. And, as everyone knows, perception is reality!

- **Relatable Branding**

People tend to identify with companies that share their values and ideals. Your customers should be able to identify your brand by how it is presented and what it says about your company and your culture.

- **Stay True to Your Brand**

While the logo, colors, and brand messaging are important, they will all be for nothing if you do not meet your client's expectations.

Broken promises are one of the reasons most brands end up losing customer trust. Your slogan should be a truism of what you have to offer, not just a catchy phrase.

### *Defining Your Ideal Client (Avatar)*

The use of the word avatar has been around for a very long time, and originally is was used as a term in Hinduism to represent the material manifestation of a deity. The business world began using the word to indicate creating a manifestation of your ideal customer.

Defining your avatar will help you determine how to fine-tune your business to attract specific people. Think about it in terms of back in the day (when you were single) you had very specific things you were looking for in a long-term partner. You went out on dates to discover if the person in front of you was what you were looking for – you asked questions, you did activities, and then you assessed if the person in front of you was truly who you were looking for!

For our purpose here and now, let's define an avatar as a person (singular) who embodies your perfect customer: they are the person who you are creating your business for, so that what you have is so compelling that they cannot help but buy.

You can't start and grow a successful business if you don't know WHO you're doing all of that for.

Let's look at a comparison so you have an idea of what defining your own avatar might look and sound like.

What an avatar is not:

"My avatar is anyone who might need my project." (Always avoid using generic words like 'everyone' or 'anyone'.)

Here is an example of what an avatar description could sound like:

"My avatar is 25-35 years of age, is female and works a full-time 9-5 job, has a family with 2 children and finds themselves frustrated and feeling alone every day because they don't know where to find the product that I'm going to provide them about X that will solve their Y issue."

The more specific you can get about the details of your ideal customer, the more successful your business will be! When you can accurately pinpoint a problem that you can solve, and you get that message out to the correct audience (your avatar) business becomes easy. When you 'pitch' and you try to convince someone that they need what you sell – that is when business gets hard.

The following worksheet should help you in defining your Avatar.

## *Define Your Prospects*

***Who is your prospect?***

Pretend your prospect is sitting across from you right now....define them in great detail. How old are they? What gender? What do they like and dislike? Where do they live? Are they married, do they have kids?

***What does your client/prospect REALLY want?***

What are their 'inner core' desires? What are their HOT points?

***What are their top fears and frustrations?***

What makes them mad? What do they worry about? What keeps them up at night?

***What are their top wants and desires?***

What is the outcome that they really want in whatever area of their lives that you are involved in? What are they really after? What is the end goal they think they want?

***Does your prospect know all about what you offer?***

What else does your product/service offer that your prospect does not know about? What else are others using it for? Could be using it for?

***How did you find or create your product/service/solution?***

The bottom line is this – the more you know about your ideal client, the more successful you will be! Once you know who your ideal customers are, the next step is making sure they know that you have the answer to the questions that they are asking.

### *Creating a Buzz*

Business owners are always chasing after the 'buzz' – that 'coveted cascade of conversation' that can drive social media traffic and sales. However, keep in mind that word-of-mouth marketing isn't something you can force. There is not one strategy that works for everyone - you must find ways to get people talking (with enthusiasm) in a positive way about what you do and what you have to offer.

The first step, of course is offering an outstanding product or service and secondly, to excel at customer service. But assuming you already have these two critical pieces in place, what else can you do to get people talking?

Jayson Demers, Founder of AudienceBloom, has created a list of free or low-cost ways to not only attract attention but also generate excitement about your brand.

**1. A creative marketing message (also known as a 'hook')**
A marketing hook is simply a short message intended to grab attention and start people talking and leave them wanting more. It can be:

- A short phrase that illustrates your unique value proposition
- A unique offer or a catchy jingle
- A list of important benefits.
- Some examples could be:

A restaurant: "We offer authentic Italian pizza until 10pm....or until the dough runs out."

A gym: "The only ladies' only fitness facility in the city."

A lead generation website: "Find out the secret to closing 80% of your deals by downloading this free guide."

Note: While you want your hook to be attention-grabbing, avoid using hype. Hype makes promises you can't keep, while a hook clearly articulates what's great about your brand or product.

**2. Limited Offers**
Test out wait lists for new products, services and events. Offer "limited" seating at webinars and live events. During busy times, put clients on a wait list for your services rather than telling them you'll get in touch when you have an opening. This presents you as a business that is in demand and the 'scarcity' concept will make 'fence sitters' take action. (Make them afraid they will miss out!)

**3. Teasers**
Teasers, hints, sneak peaks...they can be called by many names. The point is that by sharing enticing details of an upcoming product or promotion, you pique interest and leave people wanting more.

Build up anticipation by hinting at what's to come. For instance, instead of simply posting a contest on social media, start hinting at it in the week or two prior. Drop bread crumbs of information to give your followers a chance to anticipate what you have in store – and make them 'gobble' it up when you finally make it available.

**4. Transparent Communication**
In a perfect world, the concept of transparency wouldn't generate a buzz. However, because of its relative scarcity, being transparent can set you apart from the competition. When it comes down to it, being transparent simply means engaging in honest, forthright communication.

People want to buy from those whom they know and trust. Being transparent is a key ingredient for building this trust. Be open with your communication and be accountable for everything.

**5. Free PR**

Many small businesses struggle with knowing how to get their name out into the popular media. Getting mentioned in a national magazine or website can seem unlikely or even impossible.

A free PR tool like **HARO** (Help a Reporter Out) can help you get free publicity on a scale that small business owners of the past could have only dreamt of. Simply sign up to receive daily digests of media queries, and then respond to the ones that are relevant to your business. This is a great way to get quoted or mentioned in well-known media outlets.

**6. Borrow credibility from influencers**

If you have a relatively new business, you haven't had a chance to build up credibility within your industry. Connecting with influencers in your niche can help by lending you credibility until you have your own.

Find ways to connect and engage with influencers online. Share and retweet their content or reach out to them via email. Mention or tag them in posts and participate in discussions on their social media or blog posts.

**7. Give-Aways**

Eco-friendly diaper retailer The Honest Company has only been around for a few years, but some estimate that the company, founded by actor Jessica Alba, is now worth a whopping $1 billion US.

If you look at the history of how The Honest Company grew, a big part of their success can be attributed to the use of 'freebies' and samples, all used as an online marketing initiative. Through offering completely free products (pay only shipping), the company has been able to generate significant buzz around their brand. And it was all that buzz that has helped them reach the much-coveted and ever growing Millennial market. The free stuff created the buzz and got Millennials to realize that they were eco-friendly, economical and easy to purchase online – all things Millennials prize!

Generating buzz for your brand doesn't have to be expensive, but it does require some out-of-the-box thinking. While it can mean subjecting yourself to risk, for those who are creative and brave enough to try, the rewards can be priceless.

Marketing and generating buzz are some of the most challenging aspects of running a business. You need loyal customers – paying ones – to be successful. There might be people out there just waiting for your product, but you first have to get their attention. At the end of the day, if no one knows about you your business will not survive.

Buzz or word-of-mouth marketing is best described as "people talking about you." Has a friend recently recommended a restaurant or a hairdresser or told you to watch a crazy YouTube video? Has a business connection suggested a new online service that will help you with accounting? That's people talking about companies. That's creating a buzz.

"Run an advertising campaign for a week, and the campaign is gone on Monday. Vanished. You can't find it because it's run, and it's over.

But get people talking on blogs and message boards, and it stays there FOREVER!" – Mark Hughes, BuzzMarketing

***How to Generate Buzz and Connect with Influencers***

It seems like magic, but buzz is something you can generate yourself. How do you get people to talk? The first step is to differentiate yourself. If you do what every other company does, you're not worth talking about. If you're running a cleaning company in a small town and your competitors all operate in the same way with the same price points, then work to set yourself apart. Write an article for the local website, make a presentation at your children's elementary school, create a beautiful website, or offer rebates and discounts. Do SOMETHING out of the ordinary that will get you noticed.

Keep in mind that storytelling is key. Even if your company sells a boring product or service, you can tell stories that set you apart. If your company started because you lost your job or wanted to create a product for your children, talk about it with honesty and transparency. Everyone loves a good story—especially the press- so make sure to have a few in your arsenal.

If you want people to tell your story, write about you, praise you on review sites, and talk about you to their friends, then you better figure out how to talk about yourself and your company. Your job is to connect with influencers – to get the word out about your company. It's all about doing things that get people talking and getting people to write about it. The more exposure on blogs the better.

You want to email and pitch the right bloggers and reporters to let them know about something interesting. That's the key – something INTERESTING. You don't pitch the same old story - you pitch a story with relevant information that the blogger or reporter can turn into a great story. The more pitches you put out, the more people you're in front of. Staying consistent is key because you want to develop a cycle of getting the right stories to the right writers at just the right time.

### *Prioritize Customers*

Customers are the ones who will recommend you to their friends and on the web, so it's in your best interest to treat them well. It goes beyond creating a great product—you should have stellar support, build exceptional relationships, and go above and beyond your duty.

To entice and retain customers try different things like:

- Write handwritten thank you notes
- Send out personalized gifts
- Follow them on social media sites (Twitter, Facebook Google+, etc.)
- Offer promo codes and generous rebates
- Write about customers on your blog
- Use customer's services when appropriate and talk about it on appropriate social media
- Be your own ambassador at networking events

### *Tools To Build Buzz*

The following list includes various online sites that can assist you in 'building buzz'.

**BuzzStream** - Track conversations with writers, including email and social media, and the articles they write.

**TweetDeck** - For creating feeds of reporters/bloggers and better social media management.

**Cision** - Reporters/journalists/bloggers contact information – basically one giant database to comb through.

**Google Alerts** - Put in search terms and keywords to track as they appear on the internet.

**Newsle** - Interesting startup that tracks when you appear in the news. If you're constantly quoted, it's a good service to try.

Help A Reporter Out (HARO) - One of the easiest ways to see what reporters need help on and what stories they're currently working on.

***Go 'Off Line' and Read Some Books***

In the information age there are many authors who are writing about how to promote your business online. You need to compile a list and begin systematically working down the list – here are a few to get started.

**Viral Loop** by Adam L. Penenberg

There's all this talk about "going viral," but what does that actually mean? Well, according to Adam L. Penenberg, viral loops are user-generated cycles of growth. As people keep talking about an established brand, the brand gets more and more traction. We feel that Viral Loop is a must-read. Our philosophy about buzz is right in line with the ideas in this book.

**BuzzMarketing** by Mark Hughes

Generating buzz is much more effective and far cheaper than traditional strategies. If you get people talking about some interesting things you've done, you can gain customers for life. Mark Hughes tells anecdote after anecdote about how marketing with buzz propelled all sorts of companies to success.

Word of Mouth Marketing by Andy Sernovitz

Andy Sernovitz doles out tips on Wordofmouth.org, but he's also got this amazing book that'll help you master word of mouth marketing. This guide is hands-on, straightforward, and pretty funny. Sernovitz prioritizes usable techniques that will get people talking.

### *Get On Social Media*

Social media isn't just for kids. In fact, the one of the fastest growing age brackets on Twitter is the 55 to 64 age bracket. (Let's hear it for Baby Boomers!)

Pretty much everyone is using social media sites like Twitter, Facebook, LinkedIn, Instagram and Pinterest. Both businesses and individuals love to be connected. When something happens, people are buzzing on these sites like bees.

In order to capture social media buzz, set up TweetDeck, a platform by Twitter, and make columns of search terms to find out what people are buzzing about in your industry.

While social media is a new way to communicate for some, it does not mean the rules of communication have been suspended. You need to understand the different tools and how to use them – using the 'spray and pray' approach will not bring you success!

- Learn the Different Sites. What works on LinkedIn might not work on Facebook, Instagram or Twitter. Read up on how the sites work as well as what types of updates work best for each site.

- Don't Be Over-promotional. Share your blog posts and updates, but share other people's stuff, too. Your goal is always to help your customers. No one wants to hear you constantly talk about yourself.
- Have a Sense of Humor. Being personable and human will make you fun to follow. People don't like when social media accounts are too corporate and stiff.
- Use Social Media to Find Fans. If you've got fans, they're likely to follow you on social media, peppering your accounts with favorites and likes. It's great to have fans on board, so use your social accounts to find out who they are so you can reward them.
- Be an Active Participant. Don't just post once and forget about it. Social media is active all the time, so make sure you're consistently posting, and become part of the conversation. There is nothing worse for your online reparation than for people to find crickets and cobwebs when they come to your Facebook page.
- Get Some Software. Use Buffer, Argyle Social, or HootSuite to manage and assess your social media accounts. You can schedule updates and figure out how well you're performing.

### *You've Got to Surprise and Delight*

Effectively generating buzz can do wonders for your brand. In May 2009, the website Grasshopper went through a rebrand. They have been making it easier to start and grow a small business since 2003. Back then, Grasshopper started as just two guys with a dream and to date have served over 300,000 entrepreneurs with information and education on how to start a business.

When they rebranded and relaunched, they didn't just change their website and name. They actually sent out chocolate-covered grasshoppers!

They identified 5,000 influencers and raised 25,000 grasshoppers to cover in chocolate. Then, they sent out 5 to each influencer. They also created a YouTube video to inspire entrepreneurs as part of the campaign. It was a crazy idea- but it worked. The Grasshopper rebrand is a major example of a basic concept: People will talk if they're surprised or delighted.

If people think you're an average company with boring messaging and a stale attitude, they're unlikely to buzz about what you do. Sending gifts and thank you notes to customers, interacting on social media, coming up with great pieces of content, and promoting the cool things you do are all ways to get people talking. Of course, you have to continue to be awesome, so that they have something to talk about and share.

### *Creating Raving Fans*

According to Tony Robbins, the biggest mistake most businesses make is falling in love with their product or service, and not with their clients.

If you are too focused on your product, you might overlook what's best for your client and your product is nothing without a client to sell it to. However, when your client is your number one priority, your product becomes tailored to their interests. A happy client creates a great product.

If you focus only on the product, then you are a seller of a commodity. To create raving fans, you have to be unique. If you have differentiated your business by helping your clients solve a specific problem in a bold way, this is the key to making sure no one else in your industry even comes close to what you have to offer. Keep in mind, it is not just about being different. It is about giving so much value to your clients and customers that they would not even think about going anywhere else – and they talk about you with genuine enthusiasm and excitement to everyone they meet. (This is the ultimate definition of a 'raving' fan!)

Here are a few specific pointers from Tony Robbins on how to create clients and customers who will talk about you and refer to others (all part of creating a Buzz!)

**1. Under Promise and Over Deliver**
Handling expectations is one of the most important concepts when dealing with clients. If you continually give more than they expect, they will rave about you! Always make sure they are in a better place because of your product or service.

**2. Run your business in an open, transparent way**
If something goes wrong, tell your clients what happened. Explain, tell them how you fixed it and then explain how you are going to make it up to them.

**3. Always reward your best clients**
Give them special benefits, discounts, offers and value in addition to what your core clients are receiving.

**4. Create Continuous Positive Customer Experience**
It's called the value chain and a single break can permanently end your relationship with your client. You have to keep your eye on the ball in order to ensure continuity.

**5. Give back in whatever ways you can: to your clients, the industry and society as a whole**
When you create a reciprocal relationship, it strengthens the sense of fulfillment your business gives you It all comes down to constantly adding value to your clients. If you do this, they'll repay you with sharing the experience with everyone they know.

In simple terms, raving fans for businesses are the business' advocates. They are customers who would never consider taking their business elsewhere. That's a tall order in this highly competitive market place, but it is possible. Businesses with raving fans not only provide an exceptional product or service, they also provide exceptional customer service.

***In summary here are a few tips for ensuring you have raving fan customers:***

**1. Keep your commitments**
If you tell a customer you are going to do something, you do it. Case closed. Think about the last time you had to get your car repaired. Did you go in for an estimate, agree to the repair cost, and all of a sudden, the cost went up? Or, did you purchase an item that required shipment and you were told 2 – 4 weeks, but the item showed up on your doorstep 12 weeks later? Companies that make empty promises just to gain business usually end up going out of business.

**2. Communicate with and Educate your customers**
Whether it's a personal phone call, a mailer, or through social media, you can create raving fan customers by always keeping them informed. Let them know when new products or services are available, if a promotion is around the corner, or if there is an unexpected issue with a product so it can be repaired or replaced.

**3. Be consistent**
Do you have a favorite restaurant that you can go to and always get a great meal? Customers like to do business with companies that are consistent. It takes the guesswork out of the equation and creates loyalty.

**4. Acknowledge and fix problems**

If you avoid customer complaints or issues they will avoid you. Honoring your commitment, educating the customer on what can be done, and making sure you are consistent will keep them coming back. Chances are they will tell their friends how well you handled the problem and generate more business for you.

***The importance of Networking***

While branding and creating a buzz are important, don't discount the value of in-person networking. Martin Latman, a good friend of mine and one of the most professional networkers I know, has a favorite saying - "Although it is important to know a lot of people, it is much more important to know a lot of people who know you." Just think of networking as creating a 'buzz' in person.

Now, most professionals know the basics of networking, such as:

- Showing up in professional attire
- Having a firm handshake
- Having a nametag on the righthand side (direct line of sight when shaking hands)

However, try to avoid the rookie mistake of hitting the networking trail by running around the room at an event and shoving your business card into everyone's hand. (I have actually seen this happen!) That is the quickest way to lose credibility!

When it comes to networking, the most important step is to create your 'Memorable Marketing Message" (most people call this their 'elevator pitch' – however, I feel that people don't like to be pitched, so avoid this angle.)

Your Memorable Marketing Message should be a short and concise paragraph that clearly defines who you are and who you solve problems for (who is your avatar).

It should also include one memorable thing about your or your business – it should NOT be a laundry list of accomplishments, or events at your place or anything long and complicated.

Be sure and use the word 'help' in your message. (Remember WIIFM – everyone wants to know "What's In It For Me?)If you are known as a 'helper' then you become a business magnet.

Give them a clear picture of how you can help, a quick tag line that is memorable and above all, leave them wanting more!

***The Rules of Networking***

When you Google the phrase "rules of networking' up comes many articles that range from the top three rules of networking to 59 rules of networking. (Wow, that makes it sound like work!) As always, the best path to follow is the golden rule – treat others how you would like to be treated.

This translates into the concept of 'givers gain' or 'give before you get'. Always go into a networking situation with the view that you are going to connect with people and identify how you can help them. If you are genuine, you will make the right connections and networking will work for you. If you go in 'pitching' and trying to make sales, you will fail miserably!

For the most part, you will be successful at networking if you:

- Truly listen (don't just wait to speak.)
- Truly treat people with regard, respect and follow the golden rule.
- Truly be clear about who you want to connect with.
- You create and present a Memorable Marketing Message that emphasizes how you help people.

### *Tying it All Together*

It is important to find what you are passionate about in your business, just as it is important to know your AVATAR (your ideal client). These two concepts need to match up for magic to happen. If you truly understand your clients and truly give them what they want and need, then they will become raving fans. Raving fans then help your business create a buzz which gets the attention of more clients for you to delight, and so it goes ever upward.

To summarize, always follow the golden rule in creating a buzz and creating raving fans. Always treat others as you would like to be treated – and then add something extra!

# Chapter Eight

## Putting It all Together

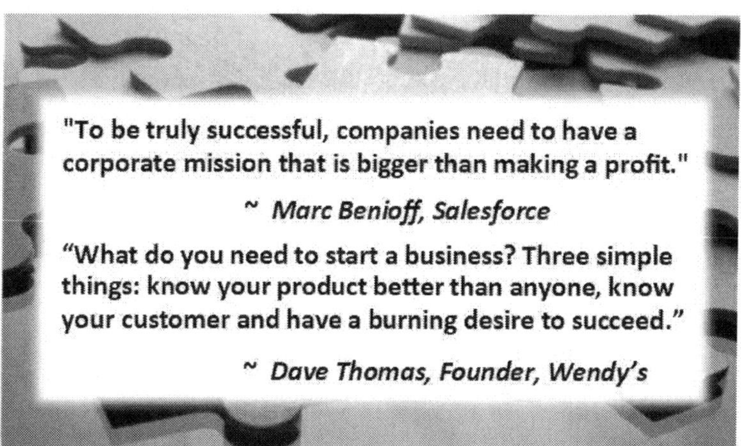

"To be truly successful, companies need to have a corporate mission that is bigger than making a profit."
~ Marc Benioff, Salesforce
"What do you need to start a business? Three simple things: know your product better than anyone, know your customer and have a burning desire to succeed."
~ Dave Thomas, Founder, Wendy's

Often when business owners complain of confusion, what they are really suffering from is being overwhelmed! Wearing too many hats can be the root cause of confusion because you end up being too tired to see the forest through the trees as you try and cover all the bases.

## Picture Perfect Business Success

We have covered much ground in how to get clarity in your business by defining your passion (what is your why) create your vision of where you want to go (creating the picture on the box) and setting out strategy and goals (mission).

***Putting the Puzzle Together***

Remember our discussion in the beginning about put together a 1,000-piece puzzle? Everyone has a different method for approaching such a complex project. Some people sort out all the edge pieces first and build the frame, others will sort the pieces into color piles, while others will start in one corner and work outwards.

There are many paths to creating a successful business. However, all successful businesses begin with a clear vision and mission. If you don't have the picture on the box, it is almost impossible to put together a 1000-piece puzzle, no matter what your method is for putting it together.

However, while I have laid out a path for going from confusion to clarity in business with specific actions needed for building a successful business, the most important points are contained in chapter four. THE most important point that I can make in your journey from confusion to clarity is learning how to enjoy the journey and taking care of yourself.

And, if you stopped and thought about it, you would realize that many of the points in this book are things that you already know. This reminds me of one of my favorite stories in The Wizard of Oz, when Glenda the Good Witch of the North points out to Dorothy that she had the power to return home all along. You do know how to get from confusion to clarity in your business – you just needed to be reminded of the steps and motivated to begin the journey down "the yellow brick road".

***Daily Motivation***

Motivational coach Barry Gottlieb encourages us to take in only positive and nourishing ideas for the first two hours of every day. Start your day with your own vision, not with the newspaper (or on-line news, depending on your preference.) It is also a good idea to actually say your vision, mission and value statements aloud each day, first thing in the morning.

***Here's why this is important:***

When we read something aloud, this activates both sides of the brain. The left side is logical-it rationalizes, but there's no passion and often creates negativity and resistance. The right side is the source of emotion and motivation. Emotion is not always practical, but when we read a purposeful, practical and passionate statement aloud, it hits both sides of the brain and brings both halves of the concept together, making it stronger.

When you stop and think about it, motivation is much like exercise - the more you do it, the stronger you get at it. The same goes for finding your passion each morning. Remind yourself why you are doing your business and it will be much easier to get up and get going in the morning. (Even if it's Monday!)

Stephen Covey, author of The Seven Habits of Highly Effective People, teaches us to put "first things first." So, if you begin every day by reciting your vision, mission and value statements that will always keep you focused on what matters most to you.

Alyssa Gregory is a small business expert and founder of the Small Business Bonfire, a blog, recourse center and online community for entrepreneurs. She understands that getting motivated (and staying there) is a very important part of turning confusion into clarity and getting to success in business.

Getting and staying motivated is vital, whether you're starting a new venture, or managing the day-to-day operations of your business. According to Gregory, lack of motivation can chip away at your self-confidence, and ultimately hurt your potential for success. The more motivated you are, the easier it will be to tackle ambitious goals and reach higher levels of success in your business.

In one of her blogs, Gregory outlines tips for how to get motivated, climb out of a slump and the build the momentum needed to reach your target.

**1. Entrench Yourself in a Goal**
While lack of motivation may not be related to a specific goal, having a goal can often help you get motivated. (Remember SMART goal setting?) is one way to outline your objectives, clarify the importance of the goal, and create an action plan for achieving it. If you are able to break down long-term goals into weekly or even daily action steps, the progress you make every day can help you build momentum and get motivated to keep the process moving.

**2. Relive Past Successes**
Do you remember what it felt like to reach an accomplishment, hit a significant milestone or make an important decision? Spend some time thinking about the process you went through, the work you put in and that sweet taste of victory. Reliving some of your best moments can get you over the hurdle and into action.

**3. Find Inspiration in Someone Else**
There will always be others who have walked the path before you, faced challenges and emerged victorious.

Spend time appreciating the drive and determination of others and exploring how they overcame the challenges they faced on their journeys can be motivating. This can also give you some creative ideas for getting through the challenges you're facing by borrowing a page out of their book.

**4. Try a New Approach**

Progress often results in routines and that can bring boredom; and boredom can cause a loss of motivation. If your routines are causing you to lose your fire, it may be time to shake things up a bit. Try altering the way you do things, when you do them, how you do them and even how you think about them. Start to question your standard processes and introduce a new way of thinking to get past complacency. It can be as simple as taking a new route to the office.

**5. Find an Accountability Partner or Coach**

Having someone there to encourage you, support you and challenge you can be an effective way to get and stay motivated. When you make a commitment to someone else to do something, you're no longer struggling along on your own. You have someone else counting on you, and most of us feel increased motivation to act when there is a chance we will disappoint someone other than ourselves. Being accountable for having said you will do something is very powerful.

**6. Psych Yourself Up**

Ultimately, motivation must come from within. The best way to get motivated is by figuring out what gets you up and gets you moving. You can try your favorite music, positive thinking, celebrating success, and creating a personal mantra. When you've found an activity that results in a boost in motivation, and makes you excited to take the next step, you have found your own motivational secret to keep you excited about your business.

Remember, saying out load and writing it down are both powerful ways to keep focused on your positive motivation.

***Concentrate on Your Entrepreneurial Spirit***

Have you ever stopped to ask yourself why people start businesses? The simple answer is that they have the entrepreneurial spirit.

In her book "Unstoppable" leadership coach Kelly Roach answers the question "What is an entrepreneurial spirit?" with:

- It is questioning everything and always asking yourself if there is a better way.
- It is knowing the reason why you do what you do and being extremely intentional about every component of your life.
- It is making bold, empowered decisions in your life that could potentially risk failure, time, embarrassment, and money because you know that status quo is not enough for you.
- It is not allowing someone else to 'assign' what your time is worth but instead determining what your time is worth and acquiring the knowledge, skills and expertise necessary to get it.

She completes her thoughts on the matter by saying the most important characteristic of an entrepreneur is the willingness to take 'imperfect action.' It is being unwilling to let fear keep you 'boxed' up, and getting out there to make your vision come true.

***Summing it All Up***

You have started a business and you are now in a world of confusion – what next? Once you have realized you need to be equal parts, Entrepreneur, Manager and Technician and yet at the same time you realize you cannot wear all the hats, the next step is taking an inventory of all the confusion- what are your pain points? It is lack of money? Lack of talent? Lack of clients?

Getting clarity in business is an important first step along the journey to a successful business. Remember, clarity starts with you, the business owner, and goes straight to the heart of why you are a business owner and what is the business you are in. Clarity means that you will make easier and better decisions - lack of clarity breeds muddled decisions.

Defining what you want the future of your business to look like is not easy. Working on clarity forces you to reflect and really understand what is important to you personally and to your business. What is your passion? What is your WHY?

Discovering your passion and putting it into practical terms is the best way to begin creating the clarity needed to ensure your business is successful. Remember the infamous Cheshire Cat, who appears in Alice in Wonderland? He gave us a true window on wisdom when he said "If you don't know where you are going, any road will get you there."

Do you remember the number one road block to creating the life of your dreams? The number one roadblock is not knowing exactly what you want! There are millions of choices and countless paths down which we can travel.

So, to begin painting the picture on your puzzle box (creating your vision statement) you need to have a clear idea of what you like, what you enjoy and where you are ultimately going with your life, both personally and professionally.

Your vision statement should be clear, concise and to the point – and it should have significant meaning for you as it will outline how you help people, what value you offer to them and how to will deliver your value. It should outline how you help people, the value you offer to the world, and what you plan to achieve as a business.

***A Vision Statement is:***

- Aspirational, in that is it about your goals for the future
- Inspirational, as it provides meaning and direction for your day to day work
- Motivational, as it will provide a reason for you and your staff for the work that you do.

Your vision statement should have your business values, business goals, strengths and opportunities clearly defined. It is your business story, a clear definition of why your business exists.

Remember to practice the art of 'being present' as you journey toward attaining clarity in your business. Being present it not hard – it is just simply something that we forget to practice. We let the ever growing 'to do' list overwhelm us, and the worry about not getting everything done actually becomes a fulfilled prophecy because the worry takes over and we forget to concentrate on the task in front of us. Keep it simple – be present, and just focus on one thing at a time.

So, you have defined your WHY, (your Purpose) you have created the picture on the box (your Vision) and now it's time to put together the puzzle (Mission Statement and goals). Don't forget to keep your goals SMART (Specific, Measurable, Attainable, Realistic and Timely).

Write your SMART goals down on paper. Keep them in your pocket. Refer to them frequently to check you are making progress toward achieving your goals. Make sure it is something that will get you out of bed in the morning, something that drives your passion.

Ok, you've created your picture on the box and you are now putting the puzzle together. Now it's time to communicate what is going on to the outside world. When it comes to communicating for maximum success in your business, there are two main concepts that must be made a priority – WHO are you communicating with and HOW are you communicating?

If you are trying to communicate with everyone in the same way, you are missing the boat! It is extremely important to learn how to be a 'chameleon' and adapt to any situation when dealing with employees, customers, connectors and competitors.

There are many types of personalities and communication styles. Remember, I use DiSC® in my coaching practice, an assessment tool that helps you build more effective working relationships based on an understanding of different behavioral styles. Having an understanding of behavior styles will make you a better communicator.

Your message (brand) needs to be crystal clear and memorable – and then you need to make sure that your business can deliver on the promise contained in your branding and you can differentiate yourself from the competition and stay profitable.

Once you have an established brand, it's then time to create a 'buzz'. By using social media and other online tools, you can really reach out to your audience and get them talking about you. And, of course, it is important for you to know how to talk about your business.

You need to create a Memorable Marketing Message that you can use when you are networking (and you should always be networking – every time you meet someone new – just remember, networking is NOT selling!)

### *Getting it All Done*

I can hear it now – "how do we get all this done?" Many experts in the area of time management will begin by having you 'multi-task' and give you complicated systems to use to keep track of everything. To be honest, this approach has always left me with a headache.

I was privileged several years ago to meet author and keynote speaker Neen James. She has a unique approach to getting things done called Folding Time. Her approach is that everyone has the same amount of time – 1,440 minutes each day. The trick is to always ask yourself if you what you are doing at any given moment in time is really the best use of your skills and talents. You make yourself accountable for how you choose to spend your time.

Neen James also makes a very good point that multi-tasking is not the answer – focus is really what you need! If you identify your priorities, make yourself accountable for all 1,440 minutes per day and create leverage – use systems, people and technology to the utmost so that you do not get overwhelmed – you can actually 'fold time' and find that you CAN get everything done!

I highly recommend that you get a copy of her book, "Folding Time" (available on Amazon). It is a great window on how to view time management in a totally different and much more productive way.

***Keeping it Simple***

Ok, you now have a blueprint on how to go from confusion to clarity in your business. It is time to put it to work, create the picture on the box and begin putting the puzzle together. Step by step, you can create a path that will lead you to success in your business. The secret is to:

- enjoy the journey
- keep putting one foot in front of the other
- visualize the end result, and
- ask for help if you need it!

***Visualizing Picture-Perfect Success***

One of the keys to achieving your goal or purpose in life is to have a clear image of it, and so it is in Golf. The clearer the visualization of yourself achieving that goal, the closer and the more passionate you are going to be about it. In golf, visualization is one of the most important things.

**Picture Perfect Business Success**

Tiger Woods used to say that he can still see the target when he is looking at the ball. He has a vision in his mind of where he wants the ball to go. I have watched the video of his epic chip shot on the 16th hole at the 2005 Masters Tournament. You can really 'see' him visualizing his shot. He thought it through, took an imaginary shot then stepped up and took the real swing – and achieved one of the most epic shots in golf history!

So, visualize your end result. See yourself with a successful business that is Picture Perfect and devoid of confusion. Just create your picture on the box and visualize yourself putting the puzzle together until reality matches your visualization.

Enjoy the journey to your Picture Perfect Business Success!

# Resources

Chapter 1

https://www.fastcompany.com/40435072/this-is-the-state-of-small-business-failure-in-the-u-s

http://www.creativityexpert.com/

http://www.squeezedbooks.com/articles/the-e-myth-revisited-why-most-small-businesses-dont-work-and-what-to-do-about-it.html

http://sozialmonster.com/what-are-pain-points/

Chapter 2

https://www.amazon.com/What-Love-Money-Will-Follow/dp/B000GKX41Q

https://www.inc.com/melody-wilding/the-secret-to-finding-your-passion-is-the-opposite-of-what-youve-been-told.html

https://www.crunchbase.com/person/rebecca-burn-callander#section-overview

https://www.entrepreneur.com/slideshow/299687#1

Chapter 3

https://en.wikipedia.org/wiki/Think_and_Grow_Rich

https://en.wikipedia.org/wiki/The_Secret_(book)

http://blog.cimpl.com/the-sigmoid-curve-a-model-for-constant-business-growth-and-innovation

https://chrisguillebeau.com/a-brief-guide-to-world-domination/

Chapter 4

https://business.tutsplus.com/tutorials/work-life-balance-cms-27083

http://townsquareinteractive.com/2017/06/14/finding-worklife-balance-as-a-small-business-owner/

https://quickbooks.intuit.com/r/productivity/12-secrets-to-achieving-a-good-work-life-balance-as-a-business-owner/

Chapter 5

https://www.projectsmart.co.uk/brief-history-of-smart-goals.php

https://articles.bplans.com/writing-a-mission-statement/

https://www.thebalance.com/susan-ward-2946932

Chapter 6

https://discprofile.com/what-is-disc/overview/

https://www.personality-insights.com/tip-remember-there-is-a-big-distinction-between-manipulation-and-deception/

https://www.goodreads.com/book/show/17131033-sticking-points

Chapter 7

http://www.mtab.com/5-tips-for-ensuring-you-have-raving-fan-customers/

https://www.amazon.com/Word-Mouth-Marketing-Companies-ebook/dp/B007Y7A50W/ref=sr_1_1?s=books&ie=UTF8&qid=1380912876&sr=1-1&keywords=word+of+mouth+marketing

https://grasshopper.com/resources/jump-starting-and-growing-your-business/marketing-and-buzz/

Chapter 8

http://www.smallbusinessbonfire.com/motivate-yourself/

http://kellyroachcoaching.com/book

http://www.wanapgolf.com/visualization-golf/

https://neenjames.com/keynotes/#topic-2

28816162R00080

Made in the USA
Columbia, SC
26 October 2018